T0384387

BETWEEN BORDERS, BEYOND BOUNDARIES

BETWEEN BORDERS, BEYOND BOUNDARIES

STRATEGIES FOR AUTHENTIC BUSINESS ENGAGEMENT

IN AN INTERCONNECTED WORLD

MURALY SRINARAYANATHAS

Forbes | Books

Published by Forbes Books, Charleston, South Carolina.
An imprint of Advantage Media Group.

Forbes Books is a registered trademark, and the Forbes Books colophon is a trademark of Forbes Media, LLC.

Printed in the United States of America.

10 9 8 7 6 5 4 3 2 1

ISBN: 979-8-88750-416-2 (Hardcover)
ISBN: 979-8-88750-417-9 (eBook)

Library of Congress Control Number: 2024915199

Cover photo by David Suh, David Suh Photography. https://davidsuhphotography.com/
Cover design by Matthew Morse.
Layout design by Megan Elger.

This custom publication is intended to provide accurate information and the opinions of the author in regard to the subject matter covered. It is sold with the understanding that the publisher, Forbes Books, is not engaged in rendering legal, financial, or professional services of any kind. If legal advice or other expert assistance is required, the reader is advised to seek the services of a competent professional.

Since 1917, Forbes has remained steadfast in its mission to serve as the defining voice of entrepreneurial capitalism. Forbes Books, launched in 2016 through a partnership with Advantage Media, furthers that aim by helping business and thought leaders bring their stories, passion, and knowledge to the forefront in custom books. Opinions expressed by Forbes Books authors are their own. To be considered for publication, please visit **books.Forbes.com**.

To my Mom and Appa who gave me the world.

*To my wife, Dasha, and my family, friends,
and colleagues who have nurtured my world.*

To my children, Sofia and Leonardo, whom I give my world to.

CONTENTS

"You are not a drop in the ocean. You are the entire ocean in a drop."

–RUMI

ACKNOWLEDGMENTS

I WOULD LIKE to acknowledge and thank all the individuals who have contributed to my growth and success throughout my life. From mentors and teachers, who have shared their wisdom and knowledge, to colleagues and friends who have provided support and collaboration—your influence has been profound.

I am grateful to the wonderful people in all the organizations and businesses I have worked with over the years. Your partnership and collaboration have been instrumental in my journey.

Thank you all for being a part of my life and for shaping me into the person I am today.

INTRODUCTION

I BELIEVE IN seven-year cycles. Each cycle begins with the knowledge that it is time to do something new. In my life, each cycle has been marked with beginnings and endings. I have learned that the sooner you embrace the closing of a phase, the better momentum you can gain in the next one.

As someone who has lived in eight countries on three continents, I have learned firsthand that the East and the West have very different perspectives. However, I have also witnessed how countries that embrace global thought, as opposed to Western thought, are setting themselves up to survive and thrive in unpredictable ways. In this book, I share my observations from a unique third-culture perspective.

I was raised as what you might call a "third-culture kid." By this, I mean a child who grows up in a culture different from the one in which his or her parents grew up. The coinage of this term is credited to American sociologist Ruth Useem (1915–2003), who used it in her studies on expatriates living in India.

I have a lot to learn and still have a long way to go, as do we all. This book comes at a time when I almost feel like I have no choice but to write it. I could never have written it when I was in my twenties or even thirties. I have noticed that people tend to be sponges until they hit their forties, absorbing and learning so much. Something changes around the fourth decade of life. We come into a space where our relationship with the world shifts, and we become founders instead of just entrepreneurs. We become leaders instead of followers. We seek to make an impact in the world as we are between watching our children grow and our parents age.

Today, I am moved with a deep recognition that time is short. I won't live forever, but my actions are clearly beginning to affect my children and those who come behind me. I know how important it is to share my experiences and contribute what I know before I move into the next phase of my life. If we can come together globally—while still thinking locally—we can all make a great impact, no matter where we are from.

I have scaled businesses successfully and unsuccessfully around the world, including Priyo Communications, Computek College, and 369 Global. I have always used the First Principles way of thinking, as in physics, where we focus on the core elements of an organization or mission and then build it up from there. We start with what people actually want and then create the structure that will give them that exact thing.

As a leader, I have always believed that grassroots are best. If you want to succeed sustainably, you need to build from the ground up to gain consumer insights. There is no single formula to guarantee you can reach people. Rather, there is an approach that any organization can take that will always set them up for success. Whether a large institution, corporation, or government, it's about thinking locally.

The North American marketplace is increasingly diverse. In this book, I'll challenge business leaders to embrace the idea that Western thinking is only one of many perspectives in the global marketplace, and that Western thought can contribute—but must not dominate—

the approach to gathering consumer insights and connecting to the intended consumer culture.

I hope to provide consumer insights to North American companies hoping to expand their reach into new markets as well as companies looking to enter North American markets. In my career, I have embedded myself in a variety of communities and regional markets to learn the impact of local nuances. I have learned the importance of delineating between Global South versus Global North societies. This includes those within Global South communities and those from the Global North whose antecedency is in the Global South (e.g. diaspora markets). For example, selling to customers in Sri Lankan communities differs in distinct ways from Bangladeshi communities. What about marketing to a Bangladeshi in Bangladesh, versus a Bangladeshi in England, versus a second-generation Bangladeshi in England? What about a Bangladeshi in Canada? France? The US? They all may have a connection to Bangladesh, but they are all distinctly different.

In most surveys or "Know Your Customer" (KYC) applications, these populations would identify as "other" and, as a result, you wouldn't gain any insights at all. I have the experience of marketing to all the "Bangladeshi" examples I listed, and I can tell you that it was similar but also very different. The differences may be minor, but they matter immensely, and they would not be understood without thinking locally.

Thinking locally means recognizing that there are real differences among people in regions, and that each local culture has its own unique and niche features. Thinking locally means learning how to listen to begin understanding the potential market. Thinking locally means using data in a way that is efficient and productive. Thinking locally means recognizing that the global economy is also a series of local economies.

Real insights are gained through authentic connection and understanding. I have witnessed as organizations and corporations learn how to listen to the consumer markets and communities they are trying to reach. When this happens, their success at reaching people grows exponentially. This act of listening requires the ability to appreciate and celebrate diversity and cultural differences, which is more than just using buzzwords. Social media and other marketing tools can build trust, but only if the consumer feels they are being heard and understood.

This isn't just a North American phenomenon. There are many Asian companies that think they should use a Western business approach when entering a market. For many large corporations, reaching into previously untapped markets is appealing and necessary to expand into the global marketplace.

Yet, time and again, Western corporations have found that their traditional marketing methods have failed to build their brands in niche and local communities. As a young entrepreneur, it can feel like you are constantly getting advice from everyone. Sometimes, it's hard to know who to listen to because it can feel like they are all saying everything except what you really want and need to hear. I really like what my brother, Lavan Srinarayanadas said, "You can't engage with everyone in the exact same way and expect the same result."

That is great advice and the reason I wrote this book.

Start a huge, foolish
project, like Noah ...
it makes absolutely
no difference what
people think of you.

—RUMI

CHAPTER 1

SEEING THE TREES FOR THE FOREST

AFTER MANY YEARS away, I finally returned to Asia. It was a business trip that brought me back to Malaysia, after more than a decade away. For a kid who grew up on three continents before the age of seven, and would continue to travel around the world, I felt like I was coming home.

As I walked the once-familiar streets, I was delighted by the bright colors and symphony of sounds. In the stream of people and vehicles, I noticed with increasing awareness that flashes of green seemed to be everywhere. On jackets, helmets, bikes, and e-scooters, they all had the same bright logo with a single word. "Grab."

I learned that this upstart rideshare and delivery company was the brainchild of two Malaysian-born Harvard Business School graduates who started out intending to make work safer for taxi drivers in Southeast Asia. Their idea blossomed to include food delivery, courier services, and payment systems, and it has surprised the Asian business community as it proceeded to effectively edge out longstanding competitors in the marketplace such as Uber and Lyft. One of the biggest factors was including scooters in their offerings, a mode of transportation that locals were already very accustomed to using and seeing on the street. There were several key factors here but essentially, listening to the local markets was the key.

No matter where on earth I travel, I am always thinking in this way. It gives me a little thrill to dig in and find out exactly why these Davids continue to slay the Goliaths. I have found that the key to these often-unexpected accomplishments is recognizing and harnessing the small and simple things that are already working within the local community. Combine those small elements, and you see massive local success that can expand in a sustainable way. Local being the most important word here. It's all about the focus on what the people on the street are doing.

I'm probably a bit of an unusual travel companion. From Miami to Paris to Dhaka, one of my favorite things to do when traveling is to just sit in one place, watching and listening to everything going on around me. While others might dash off to museums or monuments, I will find a seat in a busy square to relax, sipping tea while I watch all the people come and go.

I am fascinated by consumer behavior around the world. When I was in London a few years ago, I made a point to visit many of the tourist shops, pretending I didn't understand the many different languages being used by the people coming in and out of the shops.

Because I have traveled and lived in so many different places, I have developed the ability to understand the gist of several languages. Even if I'm not fluent, I can usually pick up people's reactions to things. It's not too hard to tell if someone is interested in something, for example, or if they are confused or frustrated. It's a part of third-culture upbringing.

Because of this, it's easy to eavesdrop a little bit when people don't think you know what they are saying. After a few days, I gained a great deal of insight into why people made the purchasing decisions they did in that busy city. I listened to people have conversations about where to shop and where not to shop, what to buy and not to buy, and why or why not they wanted to return.

I really enjoy learning more about local consumer behavior and the factors that influence buying decisions, such as education level, interests, background, and amount of free time. As a business person, I'm looking at what businesses do that works. At the end of the day, it's all about their business framework that gives a competitive advantage. How is one restaurant's customer service different from another, for example? I noticed in Malaysia that the highly popular, twenty-four-hour street food Mamak (which means *uncle*) restaurants all have water misters positioned to cool customers off as they come and go. What a brilliant way to address the heat of the country and provide great value to their customers.

HARD-WON WISDOM

I am fascinated by the nuances of culture. Some people call people like me "third-culture kids." My ethnic origin is Tamil Sri Lankan, but I was born in London, UK. By the age of seven, I had lived on three continents.

My parents, Navaratnam and Kalawathy Srinarayanathas, both left Sri Lanka in the seventies and met as students in the UK. My father studied engineering, and my mother studied nursing and then began her career. My father told my siblings and me stories about his time at university. People left Sri Lanka for the UK to study as early as the 1950s, and then during the 1980s when riots began, most of the migrating class were refugees escaping genocide. My father devoted a great deal of his time to helping the refugee Tamil-speaking community settle themselves in London. He was working as a mortgage agent at the time, so he helped them buy homes. (The value of those properties now is astronomical!) His example of giving back to the community helped me in terms of my business mindset.

There are key things that I understood at that young age, obviously not all of them consciously. I experienced that there was a huge world out there. I watched as my father did business globally, but always participated locally in making sure he was giving back. I believe that the first seven years of life are fundamental in terms of your understanding of the world, and I am extremely grateful that my first years of life were full of so many rich experiences and relationships. When I was born, my parents were still trying to get on their feet, so I was able to live in Sri Lanka with my grandparents and their daughters— my aunts. They built a relationship with me that has influenced my entire life.

My first birthday with my grandparents—Bottom row:
Vellupillai Navaratnam (L), Pathini Navaratnam (R)—
Top row: Vathsala Ratna (L), Srisala SriRanjan (R)

I returned to London when I was almost two years old and stayed there until my father sent me to Winnipeg, Manitoba, Canada. I went by myself to visit my aunt for a summer when I was six years old. When I returned, my parents had started producing films in India, so my brother, sister, and I all went along and traveled most of South India. It was wonderful until my parents sent me back to Winnipeg. My grandparents, who I lived with early in Sri Lanka, had also moved to Winnipeg with their youngest daughter, and I would go on to live with them until I was almost twelve. Confusing? Well, think about how confused I was for the first fourteen years of my life.

Unlike major cities like Toronto, in Winnipeg, there weren't many immigrants at the time. I was one of very few kids in the entire school of five hundred who was not white. I remember my Irish friend, Tadgh, once came up to me and said, "Do you know what your people have done to my people?"

Here I was, a brown kid with a British accent in Winnipeg, Manitoba, and I had no clue what he meant by "your people." I know now that he didn't mean Tamil people. He meant British people and their history with Ireland. But I didn't understand that because I didn't have a sense of identity at that age.

From the age of seven until I was twenty-one, I remained in Winnipeg. I lived with my grandparents and aunt alone until I was twelve, and then my mom, brother, and sister came from India, and we all lived together until I left at twenty-one.

From a very early age, I had to figure out how to connect with these different cultures. Without even knowing it, I learned to embed myself in the community where I lived, then I could interpret what I learned from the people around me, and finally, I could act in ways that allowed me to connect very quickly with others. It was a simple necessity if I wanted to fit in, which matters a great deal when you're a teenager.

Because of a financial assistance program, I was able to attend St Paul's High School, an all-boys, Jesuit private school. I loved it. It was very formal and structured, even to the point where we all had to wear suits. The slogan was, "Be a man for others." I appreciated the emphasis on giving back to the community because that was already a part of my family identity.

But it could be a little tough to be one of the "poor" kids in comparison to some of the wealthier student body. At lunch, everyone would purchase hot meals from the school, and I would have to eat my bologna sandwich and drink my little packet of juice. I was hungry to fit in.

I decided I wanted to make some extra money so I could start buying lunch like everyone else. My father had a whole lot of bags that he had brought back from China—little duffle bags with Nike, Puma, Adidas, and other brand-name logos printed on them. He had purchased them for $0.25 over there, so I offered to buy them from him for a dollar each. Then, I took those bags to the locker room and sold them for $15.00 each.

This is the first time the entrepreneurial drive emerged in me. It was also when I realized that business could mean so much more than money. Selling the bags wasn't about money. I just wanted to have a great lunch, and this was the method by which I thought I could do that. It also gave me a way to connect with the other boys. I met my very best friend negotiating a sale in that locker room.

My father was running several different businesses at that time, which meant he was so busy that he couldn't come to my basketball games and other school events. I decided that I would go and get a job so he wouldn't have to support me. That way, he could spend more time with me and my siblings. I started hauling garbage, working as a dishwasher, then a waiter, then a bartender. Anything that I could do to make money was worth it to me if I could find a way to spend time with him. It worked to some extent, but then he left Canada to start a business in Bangladesh, which meant even less time with him.

I graduated high school and went to university in 1996. I didn't have much of a plan, but like most South Asian households, the options were doctor, engineer, or lawyer (the IT world wasn't a thing yet). I chose lawyer because I thought it would be a good base for business which is what I really wanted to do.

I worked in various jobs and loved participating on student council in university, but my academic performance suffered. I remember putting a sign on the door in my room that said, "I'm going to make a thousand dollars a week."

My father saw that sign and laughed. He said, "If I pay you this much money to come to work for me, will you quit all these other jobs so you can focus better on your studies?"

I took him up on his offer and started working with him in our Winnipeg office. I quickly learned that being the boss's son didn't bring the privilege I expected it would. I came in imagining a luxurious office with my feet up on a big desk. Instead, I found myself at reception folding flyers and generally learning every facet of the operation. I had to start from the ground up. This hands-on experience taught me more than any classroom. My father was never big on words, but he was showing me indirectly that you need to understand every level of business to understand the business. I learned lessons by watching him during this time that I could never have gained in all the classes at university.

Working with Appa in Canada at seventeen

Working with Appa in Bangladesh
in my twenties

We were distributing water distillers, computers, and other products across Canada but after a big business spike, the business was not doing well. My father learned of a huge opportunity in Bangladesh, so he relocated there, and I continued with my studies.

My father had his first of three heart attacks in 2000. As the eldest child, I felt it was my responsibility to help my father in his business. I had just graduated with my bachelor of arts and had plans to enroll in a business/law program, but fate had other plans for me and so I went to Bangladesh. I was twenty-one.

My first two years in Bangladesh were brutal. The people were really nice, the country was beautiful, business was tough, and we were growing steadily. I was really happy to be learning from my father. But I cried almost every night because I missed home, and I was scared to lose the person I had become. I didn't open myself up to anyone even when they tried to reach out. I can't tell you what the exact moment was because, honestly, it was a series of events but one first step of embedding myself in my new environment was when I did my MBA.

My father always said, "If you want to learn business, come work with me, and I will show you something you won't learn in books." He was right. However, I did my MBA in Bangladesh and it provided critical insights. The insights were not necessarily on business theory. These were helpful, but it was the discussions in a class on Western Case Studies that provided insights for me on the Eastern interpretation I would hear from my classmates. They were not worried about what the "Western" kids thought of them in class because they weren't in the US. They were in Bangladesh, and they spoke boldly from their perspective.

I was given a failing grade in my organizational behavior class when the dean of the school (who was teaching the class) made a sexist comment about one of the case studies involving a female CEO. I immediately reacted. A few friends sitting nearby quietly warned me to keep my thoughts to myself, but I couldn't stay quiet. "This is ridiculous," I protested to the whole class. "This isn't how the West works!"

I actually had to switch universities after that, but I gained a valuable lesson about how this part of the world thought. It also gave me great insight into how I thought.

I wish I could remember what the dean said that day. I know it would provide more context. But the lesson is much larger. Were my thoughts the "correct" thoughts? Was I being mindful and understanding of the customs and traditions of the place I was in?

I recall it as sexist, but was it? Or was I missing the context of the place around me? My fellow classmates warned me not to say anything. Did they warn me because they thought I was right but knew I would get in trouble for speaking up against authority? Or were they encouraging me not to say anything not because they wanted to save me from getting reprimanded, but because they wanted to appease my Western thoughts and be agreeable? Or maybe in their minds, they were being kind because they knew I didn't understand the context behind the comment?

Hindsight is 20/20, and looking back on that moment now, I have a deeper understanding. At that moment, I was a young man in his mid-twenties, raised in the West, living in the East, and I had a lot to learn.

Over time, I started to thrive. We even kind of figured out how to work well together in terms of father and son, and we really built a bond, which we still have today. We failed very quickly. And we won just as quickly. That's one of the benefits of doing business in Southeast Asia. The lessons I learned from taking on those challenges are very precious to me today.

That period of my life really was essential in terms of understanding how people do business in different parts of the world. I was allowed to connect with diplomats, prime ministers, and ministers. Today, when I meet high-power leaders, I'm not nervous. It's just part of doing the job I love.

UNDERSTANDING CULTURE

One of the many things I've learned throughout my life is that everyone has a story, a unique collection of connected moments that's made them who they are and inform how they see the world. Our stories continue to be written with every new experience and every new day. When we go somewhere new, whether it's a new job, a new city, or even a new country, we're writing a new chapter of that story.

It's important to have a framework for understanding what happens when we're in new environments. Within every city in the world, whether it be Chicago, Paris, or Nairobi, there are pockets of distinct cultures. You can find places where certain customs, traits, and even language patterns are different from the rest of the city. This can be very disconcerting to visitors who come for the first time. First-time sightseers to Vancouver, for example, might be surprised at the many "student drivers" in and around the historic neighborhood of Chinatown. Or people who go to New Orleans for the first time expect to see nothing more than drunk college students and are surprised at the number of cultured, skilled jazz musicians and street artists.

This is magnified when you try to move and establish a business in a new place. In Canada, you will find Ethiopian Canadians, Tamil Canadians, Mexican Canadians, and more. I believe that when you have all of these different cultures in the boardroom, it is nothing but a good thing. Like any big city, in diversity you find the micro solutions to address the macro challenges we have globally. Including many different perspectives is crucial to solving worldwide problems.

You've probably heard people say you should network and get involved in your community. But what does that mean and why does it matter? Networking isn't just about having awkward conversations with people you don't know over coffee. We've all done that before and it's not fun for anyone. But there is value in pushing past your comfort zone anyway. These uncomfortable experiences allow us to reflect and interpret what we are encountering. When something is new, we see it with a fresh perspective and get curious.

For me, networking and getting involved with local initiatives is the key to becoming authentically connected with people and the key to feeling at home. Doing this in Bangladesh helped me understand more about where I was. It also helped me build connections and feel less isolated.

As a frequent keynote speaker, I often share the story of my struggles adjusting to the first few years in Bangladesh, and I am always approached by people who want to talk about their own journeys entering new countries. We all know what it means to feel isolated and alone. We all know what it feels like when we don't understand the world around us. I have recognized a pattern that anyone can follow that helps overcome those feelings and gives anyone who follows it a chance to be a real part of their new community.

Delivering training in Bangladesh

EMBED, INTERPRET, ACT

This pattern is a three-step approach I like to call the EIA method. It stands for Embed, Interpret, and Act. And it works. I'm living proof that it does.

Let's start with the first step: embed. We learn best when we have real connections and understanding of the people around us. Embedding begins with embracing everything about the places we are in and seeing new things as opportunities to grow, not things to be scared of. When I've embedded myself into the communities I have lived in, I've succeeded. And when I haven't, it's been very difficult. To embed is to let go of that very human urge to want everything to remain familiar. It means we get comfortable with the unknown, pushing ourselves to new limits.

Once we do that, we can then interpret the information that we are gathering. Whether it's through observing, listening, participating, or otherwise making authentic connections, we gather facts, opinions, and details about our new world. This information has the power to shape how we see everyone and everything around us, and this matters greatly because how we see the world influences our reality. We have a richer worldview, meaning we have more to offer. And that is when we can act in new ways.

I have the great fortune of being able to call Dr. Rathana Peou Norbert-Munns my friend and colleague. She is an award-winning futurist and experienced researcher with extensive global experience. She emphasizes the importance of active listening and openness as part of engaging with new cultures, which fits very well with the EIA method. She shared her philosophy:

> I believe that it's very important to be as open and active a
> listener as possible because that exposes you to the richness

of the culture you are working with. There is a part of human nature that likes the comfort to be with people that are rather similar to us, but when you do that, sometimes you will also risk to not fully embrace and dive in another country's culture and people. Embracing our uniqueness goes beyond recognizing our differences; it involves actively celebrating the diverse backgrounds and experiences that each of us brings to the table. As a simple first step, I always encourage people to try new things, like taking a cooking course in the new place or some language classes. Learn the culture and all that goes with it.

This means putting what you have learned, seen, and heard into practice. Adaptation and change is the key here. It is imperative to learn how to ask and not just what to ask. This leads to questions like: How do I use the insights I have gained? What can I learn from my improved understanding? It's important to understand that our usual approaches to doing things may not have the same impact as they did where we come from. So, we need to tweak things and create something new. Traditional Western thought is only one of many perspectives.

WHAT THIS MEANS FOR ORGANIZATIONS

I believe every organization needs diverse perspectives. Netflix is a great example of this. If you have watched over the years, they have offered more and more foreign content. They know how to focus on very niche content customized to suit their specific audiences, and it works. Imagine if every North American company learned how to interact and understand not just how to market or sell but also how not to market or sell.

They can!

I do think large corporations need to understand this. Small businesses are in an excellent position to learn this method. They can go global online, sure, but if they're looking to have a physical presence in different countries or really tap into niche markets, they really need to understand that it's not just about hiring someone from that community. They are becoming a part of that community. It means creating an organizational structure where you can go in seeking to learn and to embed yourself there. It means really opening yourself up to learning the traditions, the style of conversation, the customs. For example, in the West, we're very focused on eye-to-eye conversation, but eye contact for people in many cultures is unpleasant.

When I was a young guy first working overseas, if I was having a conversation with someone, I wanted to be lined up straight with them. I noticed they kept turning away, so I'd move to square with them. Then, they would turn away again. It was like a dance we were doing. I didn't know they were turning away to be respectful. I was just confused about how to have a meaningful conversation and trying to connect with someone who wouldn't look me in the eye.

These are the types of things you learn as you follow the EIA method. I know it can be difficult to stay positive when things are just not working out. In the coming chapters, I hope to be able to share with you concrete suggestions that will help you continue to push forward and never give up on your dreams. You have the power to write your own story, the talent to make a change, and the opportunity to make a positive impact.

Sell your cleverness and buy bewilderment. Cleverness is mere opinion.

Bewilderment brings intuitive knowledge.

—RUMI

CHAPTER 2

CONSUMER INSIGHTS: GLOBAL VERSUS LOCAL

THROUGHOUT HISTORY, FEW events have changed the world quite as profoundly as the Industrial Revolution. This era revolutionized manufacturing and trade and brought about advancements that touched every aspect of life. It was a time period when motorcars and railroads replaced the humble horse and cart, and steam-powered ships overtook sailboats and traveled to places that everyone thought were impossible to reach. Innovations like the power loom, the cotton gin, gas lighting, the telegraph, and eventually the telephone brought about what we now call global trade and interaction on an unprecedented scale.

But with all of these changes also came a lot of problems. The new wealth from factories and trade wasn't shared equally, causing huge economic gaps both within countries and between them. Nations that had been friends found themselves competing for resources and markets in ways they never had to before. This led to governments taking over lands and hurting local populations to get ahead. The early twentieth century was marked by drastic economic ups and downs, with the Great Depression of the 1930s showing just how unstable the global economy could be.

As countries struggled with these economic problems, it became clear that the world needed a stable financial system. This led to the Bretton Woods Conference in 1944, where leaders from forty-four allied nations met to create a new system to keep economies stable and prevent future crises. This meeting led to the creation of the International Monetary Fund, the World Bank, the World Trade Organization, and the European Union. These organizations still work to promote economic cooperation and development around the world.

Why do I tell you all of this?

Well, this is really how our global village came to be what it is today and has allowed us to continue the international trade practices that started hundreds of years ago. Advancements in technology, especially computing and the internet, have continued to change the global marketplace in our lifetime. The ability to coordinate complex supply chains and services across the planet means the whole world can trade in ways we never imagined a few centuries ago. The fact that I can order a smartphone designed in California, assembled in China, with parts sourced from multiple countries, and have it delivered to my doorstep within days is a testament to how interconnected and efficient global trade has become.

But there is always a downside. With each advancement, challenges have threatened to ruin the harmony that most leaders hoped to achieve in the global sphere. An example is the Cold War and Ideological Divide that took place between the US and the Soviet Union from the mid-1940s to the early 1990s. This division between the capitalist and communist had an effect on global trade and economic policies.

Individual consumer choices were also driven by propaganda that was spread on both sides. American children were taught to fear the "commies," while Russian children were taught to fear their "imperialist" enemy. The trade of goods and services was effectively frozen between these two countries for decades.

This is just one example of the thousands of other events that have shaped the modern global marketplace. The ripple effect of things like this impacts individual consumers in massive and lasting ways. Economists, business leaders, and marketers have grappled for nearly a century to understand how specific factors influence buying decisions and how to best approach new marketplaces. Can anyone really understand why people do what they do? Or why people buy what they buy?

GLOBAL VERSUS LOCAL

It can be useful to turn to the experts when trying to understand something so complex. Brace yourself a little bit because I'm going to get kind of technical. But I hope you'll stay with me because this is very interesting and useful stuff.

Jan-Benedict E.M. Steenkamp is a respected authority in the field of marketing and consumer behavior. He has made significant contributions to the understanding of global and local consumer cultures. His in-depth research and analysis provide valuable insights, and we try to understand and navigate the evolving landscape of our consumer culture in an increasingly interconnected world. Steenkamp's work provides a comprehensive analysis of consumer attitudes toward global and local consumer cultures, as well as the measurement of these attitudes.

His 2017 book, *Global Brand Strategy: World-wise Marketing in the Age of Branding,* illustrates how global brands generate value through what he calls the COMET framework: Customer Preference, Organizational Benefits, Marketing Benefits, Economies of Scale, and Transnational Innovation (Figure 1).

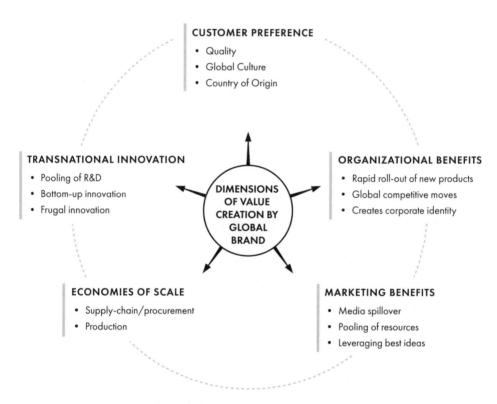

CUSTOMER PREFERENCE
- Quality
- Global Culture
- Country of Origin

TRANSNATIONAL INNOVATION
- Pooling of R&D
- Bottom-up innovation
- Frugal innovation

DIMENSIONS OF VALUE CREATION BY GLOBAL BRAND

ORGANIZATIONAL BENEFITS
- Rapid roll-out of new products
- Global competitive moves
- Creates corporate identity

ECONOMIES OF SCALE
- Supply-chain/procurement
- Production

MARKETING BENEFITS
- Media spillover
- Pooling of resources
- Leveraging best ideas

Figure 1. Steenkamp, Jan-Benedict. Global Brand Strategy: World-wise Marketing in the Age of Branding. *1st ed., Palgrave Macmillan, 2017.*

Let's break this framework down further:

CUSTOMER PREFERENCE

First, global brands give the impression of high quality. People assume that the fact the brand is global must mean it is a high-quality product because of the global acceptance and appreciation of the brand. How could a low-quality product be offered globally? Second, most consumers today prefer brands that originate from a country of origin. For example, Italian suits, tea from Sri Lanka, etc.

ORGANIZATIONAL BENEFITS

One of the biggest advantages of a global brand is the rapid rollout of products. Global brands have the ability to bring products to the marketplace quickly, without having to take into consideration how to customize them each time for a local market. In Steenkamp's book, he illustrates the organizational benefits with the example of Unilever. In the past, Unilever struggled with over five thousand new product projects attempting to cater to each local market. However, after re-strategizing the approach to global consumer markets, they reduced their products to six hundred and saw a massive improvement in sales and profit margins.

MARKETING BENEFITS

When you think about global marketing, there are huge advantages. Centralized brand guidelines and promotion at worldwide events can propel a brand to global levels. Events like the Olympics and widely popular sporting events like football can ensure a brand's global reputation and presence. To connect with local markets, partnering with a local celebrity can connect a global brand with a locally recognized one.

ECONOMIC BENEFITS

Global brands can reduce the production costs of their goods and services by outsourcing production to low-cost countries. Technology has changed some of the economics around the advantages of outsourcing and so has the increased costs of supply chains. However, there are still opportunities to optimize outsourcing.

TRANSNATIONAL INNOVATION

The cost of research and development (R&D) has skyrocketed in the West. For example, Gillette's five-blade razor blade apparently had an R&D price tag of over $500 million. The advantage as a global brand is access to global markets. Consumer insights, although different in different regions, can, if collected effectively, provide insights into global consumer preferences.

Two years after he published his book, Steenkamp published a report titled "Global Versus Local Consumer Culture: Theory, Measurement, and Future Research Directions" for the *Journal of International Marketing*. That report has had lasting implications for consumer decision-making, including the influence of national culture and of individual-level factors. In this report, Steenkamp explores the complex dynamics between global consumer culture (GCC) and local consumer culture (LCC).

The study provides some great insights for business leaders. For several decades, Steenkamp has observed a shift away from LCC and toward GCC. However, over the past few years, it appears that GCC is stalling and beginning to shift back toward LCC. This shift may be attributed to a host of factors such as the collapse of communism; the opening of markets in parts of Asia, Latin America, and Eastern Europe; and increased access to travel, telecommunication, and technology.

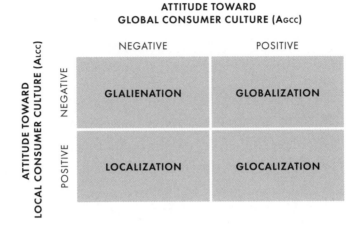

ATTITUDE TOWARD
GLOBAL CONSUMER CULTURE (Aɢᴄᴄ)

	NEGATIVE	POSITIVE
NEGATIVE	**GLALIENATION**	**GLOBALIZATION**
POSITIVE	**LOCALIZATION**	**GLOCALIZATION**

ATTITUDE TOWARD LOCAL CONSUMER CULTURE (Aʟᴄᴄ)

Figure 2. Steenkamp, Jan-Benedict. Global Brand Strategy: World-wise Marketing in the Age of Branding. *1st ed., Palgrave Macmillan, 2017.*

Figure 2 represents a typology of those various consumer responses. Steenkamp offered the following definitions for the four terms inside the boxes:

1. *Glocalization*: This term refers to the adaptation of global products and services to fit local cultures and preferences. It combines the concepts of "globalization" and "localization," indicating that while products and services may be globally distributed, they are tailored to meet the needs and desires of local consumers. This approach recognizes the coexistence and interdependence of global and local influences.

2. *Localization*: This concept emphasizes a positive attitude toward local consumer culture while having a neutral or indifferent attitude toward global consumer culture. Local-

ization focuses on preserving and promoting local traditions, customs, and consumption patterns. It involves adapting products and services to align with local tastes, values, and identities, often resisting global homogenization.

3. *Globalization*: This term describes the increasing interconnectedness and interdependence of world markets and businesses. It involves the spread of products, technology, information, and jobs across national borders and cultures. A positive attitude toward global consumer culture signifies openness to global brands, values, and lifestyles, often embracing the homogenizing effects of global market integration.

4. *Glalienation*: Although this term is less commonly used, it can be understood within the context of the figure as representing a negative attitude toward both local and global consumer cultures. This perspective reflects a sense of alienation or detachment from consumer cultures in general, rejecting both local traditions and global influences.

These definitions provide a framework to understand how consumers might perceive and engage with both local and global consumer cultures. (It can't account for all the individual-level factors, such as acculturation and personality traits, on consumer attitudes, so we will go into that later in the book.) Steenkamp's work initially proves that global cultures are becoming more homogenized, but the shift back toward LCC seems to show large parts of the world are still not ready to embrace large-scale changes. Trying to understand the current situation and changes between LCC and GCC is even more important to understanding international markets than ever before.

In summary, trying to figure out how people shop and what they value can be a real mixed bag, but it's not impossible! I share all of this because it is one of the many important studies that provide valuable insights for business leaders seeking to navigate the evolving landscape of consumer culture in an increasingly interconnected world. It is just one step toward success when moving into a new market.

Of course, we still have to remember that consumer preferences are as diverse as ever, constantly being shaped by a blend of global influences and local traditions. Because I believe in turning to experts whenever possible, I believe this is very useful information and worth the time to learn. It is very interesting and applicable to the work I have done and am continuing to do around the world.

As business leaders embrace these insights and consciously adapt to the ever-changing market dynamics, they invite greater innovation and growth in their organizations. That, coupled with optimism and a commitment to understanding and meeting the needs of diverse consumers, is the key to creating a brighter business future.

Learn the alchemy true
human beings know.
The moment you
accept what troubles
you've been given
the door will open.

—RUMI

CHAPTER 3

THE GLOBAL VILLAGE IS MORE THAN WESTERN THINKING

BUSINESS IS ULTIMATELY about people and the vibe you send out into your community. Right now, the world is this big, mixed-up place. You could be running a business from your home in Chicago, but your IT wizard might be coding away in India, and your customer service crew answering calls in the Philippines. It's like being local and global all at once. And that's something you've got to get the hang of if you want to make it in today's world.

Where do we turn when we want to learn how to do this? History is a great teacher, offering us insights and perspectives that can profoundly shape our choices and actions. Take global conquests throughout history, as an example. These were rarely just about the expansion of an empire. A great deal of study has gone into exploring how history's greatest conquerors managed to create the vast and enduring empires that they did. As it turns out, their success wasn't just about military might—it was also about embracing diversity and incorporating the best of the cultures they encountered.

Take Genghis Khan, for example. Founder of the Mongol Empire, Khan is most often remembered for his brutal military campaigns. However, he was actually quite savvy when it came to dealing with the people he conquered. He was brilliant in the strategic incorporation of the cultures he subdued. Unlike many conquerors, Khan did not seek to replace local customs or religions. Instead, he welcomed them and assimilated valuable aspects of each culture into his empire, thus enriching Mongol society and creating a mosaic of diversity that led to a flourishing of trade, technology, and ideas across his vast territories. This approach not only helped keep the peace, but it also fostered a dynamic cultural exchange across his sprawling territories.

Similarly, Alexander the Great was known for his policy of "fusion" as he blazed his way through history. Alexander the Great's expeditions through Asia Minor, Egypt, and into the heart of the Persian Empire were marked by his respect for local traditions and religions.

He actively encouraged the blending of Greek and Eastern cultures, promoting unity and cooperation and laying the groundwork for the cosmopolitan Hellenistic world that followed. Thanks to him, people from all walks of life could mingle and learn from one another in ways that were not possible before, bringing about an unprecedented cultural exchange and laying the foundations for advances in arts, science, and philosophy.

In the global village of the twenty-first century, businesses and nations that thrive are often those that embrace diversity as an asset. Modern corporations can look to these historical models to understand the value of incorporating various cultural perspectives into their operations.

Just as Genghis Khan allowed different cultures to retain their identity while contributing to the empire's common good, businesses today can take a page from Khan's playbook, welcoming employees from all backgrounds and encouraging them to share their unique perspectives and skills. Not only would this make for a more inclusive and dynamic workplace culture, but it could also give the company a serious competitive edge when it comes to innovation and problem-solving. By fostering an inclusive culture, companies benefit from a wider range of ideas and approaches, leading to creative solutions and a competitive edge in the global market.

The legacy of Alexander the Great reminds us that the fusion of cultures can lead to a richer, more cohesive society. In modern terms, this can translate into multinational companies encouraging cross-cultural collaborations that respect local sensibilities. To follow Alexander's example, businesses can develop products and services that resonate across cultural boundaries, thus expanding their reach and influence. Picture a global brand that follows in Alexander's footsteps, actively seeking out ways to connect with and celebrate the diverse cultures of its customers around the world. By showing respect for local traditions and tailoring its offerings to suit different tastes and preferences, such a brand could build a loyal following that transcends borders and language barriers.

These two historical narratives demonstrate that respect for and integration of different cultures can lead to enduring legacies. Their empires expanded not merely through conquest but also by valuing and integrating the cultures they encountered. They posed questions such as "What are the good things about your culture?" and "How can we incorporate them to coexist in a collaborative manner?" This inclusiveness allowed for the creation of some of the world's largest empires, not by imposing their own culture but by connecting and collaborating with others.

Companies that emulate these principles not only set themselves apart in the marketplace but also contribute to a more interconnected and harmonious global community. In a world that is rapidly shrinking yet increasingly diverse, the lessons from the past can illuminate the path to sustainable success and unity in the future. This is a genuine commitment to empathy, open-mindedness, and mutual understanding.

Instead of entering new markets with the mindset of cultural dominance, businesses can aim to first Embed (live and work in the culture you seek to reach), Interpret (understand and integrate local cultures), and finally Act (offer your goods or services in a manner most appropriate to the new culture). I am going to go much deeper into this in the coming chapters, but for now, this could mean altering product offerings to match local tastes, respecting cultural practices, or even adjusting marketing strategies to better align with local consumer behavior. The goal is to find a harmonious balance that respects the cultural integrity of the markets they serve while still promoting their brand and values.

In a modern business context, this approach calls for a shift away from a singular Western-centric viewpoint and embracing a global perspective that recognizes the value of diverse thought. The key to sustainable growth and harmonious global relationships is to resist the impulse to dominate and instead to engage in global thinking, just as the great historical empires did through collaboration and connection.

CULTURAL NUANCES

In my role as CEO of Computek College, I have the unique opportunity to learn from our student body, a very culturally diverse group of immigrants and newcomers to Canada. Our mission is to bridge the gap between dedicated professionals seeking employment and the organizations looking to hire them. One of the main focuses of Computek currently is to prepare our students to work in the health-care sector.

I have been amazed at the observations I have been able to make. The human body may be universally similar, yet the cultural approaches to healthcare vary significantly around the world. From the way medical care is administered to the interaction with authority figures in the healthcare setting, the differences are substantial. Unfortunately, this cultural aspect of healthcare training is often overlooked in the education of medical professionals, an oversight that we aim to address in our programs. Understanding and respecting these nuances is essential, not only for providing competent care but also for integrating more culturally appropriate skills and services into the broader framework of Canadian healthcare.

Other colleges might offer a communication course that touches on this topic, but this is entirely insufficient. While these courses may provide a basic framework for interaction, they often fall short in addressing the rich tapestry of cultural nuances that professionals encounter in healthcare settings. The education system, as it stands, seldom delves into healthcare factors such as the complexities of trauma, workplace stress, and medicine. There is no guidance on how these are perceived and managed across different cultures. Traditional curricula rarely unpack the layers of trauma that patients from diverse backgrounds may experience, failing to equip healthcare professionals with the necessary skills to address psychological wounds that are often invisible, yet profoundly impact patient care. Stress and its repercussions are viewed and handled differently across the globe, influenced by varying cultural norms and practices, and a deeper understanding of these perspectives can provide higher quality, customized healthcare.

In the realm of medicine, understanding the cross-cultural dimensions of pain management and the varying thresholds and expressions of suffering is crucial; yet, such topics are notably absent in standard educational programs, leading to a one-size-fits-all approach that overlooks the intricacies of individual and cultural differences in the healing process. In some Western cultures, patients are encouraged to express their pain openly and use what is called "the pain scale" to quantify their discomfort. However, in some Asian cultures, for example, it is customary to endure pain stoically due to cultural values around endurance and saving face. A healthcare provider who is not attuned to these cultural differences might misinterpret a patient's subdued expressions of pain as a sign that their discomfort is not severe, leading to the under-treatment of pain. Similarly, a patient from a culture that uses more expressive ways to communicate distress might be perceived as exaggerating their pain, which could result in skepticism from the healthcare provider and potential over-treatment.

I have a very personal example that illustrates the need for cultural awareness in the medical field.

When my family visited Sri Lanka recently, my wife who works as a physician at Markham Stouffville Hospital just outside of Toronto gained valuable insight that enhanced her medical practice. During her work at the hospital, my wife noticed a pattern among patients who had recently returned from trips to Sri Lanka. Many of them had wounds on their feet, and she couldn't understand why this was happening so frequently.

Our visit to a temple in Sri Lanka provided the answer. As is customary, we removed our shoes before entering the sacred space. The temple floor itself was smooth, but the path leading to the entrance was lined with rocks and pebbles. As we walked barefoot along this path, my wife realized that this was likely the cause of the injuries she had been seeing in her patients.

My father, who joined us on the trip, is diabetic, which means that any wound or injury to his feet could lead to serious complications. For diabetic individuals, even small cuts or bruises on the feet can be dangerous, as they heal more slowly and are prone to infection. In severe cases, untreated wounds can even lead to amputation. This realization was a lightbulb moment for my wife, helping her to better understand and treat her patients who had been injured during their trips to Sri Lanka.

By witnessing firsthand the cultural practices that were contributing to these wounds, my wife gained a valuable perspective that improved her ability to provide culturally competent medical care. This experience reminded us both of the importance of understanding and respecting the customs and traditions of different cultures, especially when they intersect with health and well-being.

GLOBAL THINKERS

A colleague of mine once told me that the way you do one thing translates to the way you do everything. I have been contemplating that ever since.

Western thinking is not incorrect. Neither is Eastern thinking. Rather, we need to synthesize the two. Blending East and West is what makes the global village the vibrant, thriving place we all want to live in. Again, looking to the past can help us understand exactly how we can do this. It means dropping the assumption about what some countries are like.

Daniel Bernhard has led and advised charities, foundations, and government agencies all around North America, Europe, and the

Middle East with the mission to build and deliver creative, transformational programs that advance the public good. He said:

> I think that Western businesspeople privileging Western know-how is a sort of hangover from a time when the practices in these other countries were unsafe or actually inferior to what we do now... I think we conflate the need to verify quality and safety, which is definitely important. But we should not do that with the assumption that our method is therefore the best and the safest. It's not always. Sometimes it is, but often it's not.

> At the Institute for Canadian Citizenship, we have about thirty employees from sixteen or seventeen different countries. They all bring different ideas and ways of doing things that are helpful to us. Many of these countries are less developed than Canada in some respects, but in other respects, they do a lot of things better than we do, and it helps to learn from those things. The rest of the world has changed a lot faster than our world has. We have immigrants who come to Canada from countries that raise whole cities before we can even approve a building permit.

> We often think that people who are compelled to leave, who come to find asylum, etc., have less to offer than the people who are economic immigrants or entrepreneurs. But they bring a whole other level of resourcefulness. Those societies have gone from manual labor, peasant societies to hugely advanced in many cases.

> The fact that they're moving a lot faster than us is because they've incorporated many of the things that we've learned

and then added on other things. If we just want to say that those things don't count, then they're going to leave us in the dust.

Daniel Bernhard, CEO, Institute for Canadian Citizenship, makes a guest appearance on my podcast, Third Culture Leaders, *May 2024*

Learning from the past isn't about a trip down memory lane—it's about finding the golden keys to success that have always been there. Take Peoplehood, for instance. This organization is a digital-first, relational fitness platform founded in 2022 by the team behind SoulCycle. Called "a workout for your relationships," Peoplehood was created by entrepreneurs Elizabeth Cutler and Julie Rice. It focuses on creating a space for individuals to speak freely, listen deeply, and enhance their listening skills to strengthen relationships. The goal is simply to facilitate guided group conversations on a small scale, organized by similar interests and phases of life, to improve relationships and foster connections. When you join, Peoplehood offers sessions called "Gathers," where participants engage in fifty-five-minute guided group conversations to discuss their deepest hopes, fears, and emotions.

They've created a space where folks get together, not just to sweat it out but to really connect and chat. It's all about getting people to truly listen to each other. In today's world where everyone is keen to broadcast their own stories, the art of listening is getting drowned out. But Peoplehood is trying to turn the volume down and tune into each other instead.

Understandably, the press struggled to understand what it was and why it existed. It seemed to some to echo a support group or a social club, but there were no specific boundaries that could categorize it. That didn't stop Cutler and Rice. Without knowing it, they followed the EIA method. They first Embedded themselves with their customers through SoulCycle. They Interpreted what people needed, seeing a growing disconnect among people along with an accompanying desire for human connection. Then, they Acted, setting up the "Gathers" that fill that need.

Leaders can learn from what Peoplehood is doing. We read and hear discussions all the time about the existence of multiple global consumer cultures, but in the public consciousness, the global marketplace is still dominated by Western thinking.

In the realm of professional training and employment, my other organization, 369 Global endeavors to educate, inform, and activate global thinkers. We are working to connect global thinkers to take on global challenges. Our mission extends across continents and sectors. For example, we recruit individuals in Kenya to be trained and then hired to work in the cybersecurity industry with Canadian organizations, thus enhancing global exchange.

Cyber Guard Africa Ltd., Startinev & 369 Global's Africa Hack-a-thon, United States International University—Africa, Kenya, February 2024

These prospects are eager to embrace new opportunities and are prepared to bridge any gaps in their skill set. In the past, training like this had a fundamental challenge in the expectation that individuals must assimilate unidirectionally into the Western workplace culture. While there is merit to learning the Western approach, the burden of adaptation should not be placed solely on new hires.

We are trying to facilitate a broader organizational shift to inclusivity and understanding—recognizing that cultural competence is as vital as soft skills and knowledge. In essence, businesses must move beyond a one-dimensional approach, developing new-hire training that respects and incorporates international perspectives.

EMBRACING THE DIASPORA

My friend and business partner Kumaran Nadesan was born in Sri Lanka to professional parents, similar to myself. When civil war broke out, his family also realized there was no future there and made the difficult decision to leave. They relocated while Kumaran was still very young, making him a third-culture kid who grew up living in different countries in South Asia and the Middle East. At age sixteen, his family moved again—this time immigrating to Canada, where we met in 2015.

As a teenager adjusting to his new homeland, Kumaran felt the strangeness of being both an outsider and an insider and struggled to define his identity against mainstream expectations. While he was a student at university and longing to connect more deeply with his Tamil roots, he helped create a program to connect second-generation Tamil Canadians back to their roots in Sri Lanka, with a focus on youth traveling there to teach and give back. It focused on service learning, with youth teaching English and volunteering for nonprofits while also learning about their cultural heritage.

Kumaran explained:

> We created this structured program by which second-generation Canadians who were of Tamil heritage could go back to Sri Lanka for three months minimum, and work with local community-based organizations and public sector institutions to build the capacity of these organizations to serve people in need. Over a span of four years, we sent back urban planners, engineers, physicians, teachers, and creative artists to work with communities and organizations in need. This was an early model to return the diaspora/third-culture kids who were armed with knowledge through

education and experience in the Global North, but because of their origins in the Global South, they still had those local cultural/consumer insights in terms of how do you go and actually work with these populations.

Though this program later dissolved, it powerfully shaped Kumaran's worldview. He still sees tremendous value in people with cross-cultural literacy and connections, circulating ideas, investments, and skills more fluidly in our globalized world.

In 2014, after time spent building his professional career, Kumaran felt called to rekindle the same spirit of cross-cultural exchange and diaspora-driven development impact. He co-founded "comdu.it," a portmanteau of "community" and "conduit." Similar to the one he worked on at university, this organization enabled young Tamil Canadians to engage in community development projects in Sri Lanka. The premise this time was that by bridging their hybrid identity, third-culture kids could leverage insider knowledge and empathy to drive change quickly.

During his time working with comdu.it, he saw firsthand the impact of cultural and linguistic understanding in international development work. One example was when his Tamil-speaking Canadian volunteers partnered with volunteers from the opposite side of the globe.

The Australian NGO was engaged in urban planning for a town in Sri Lanka and had deployed enthusiastic young staff from Australia and New Zealand to conduct planning and community engagement. Despite their best efforts, the project encountered challenges and suspicion from the local Tamil population during stakeholder consultations. However, the partner organization confided to Kumaran that everything changed once his team of diaspora volunteers arrived. The Tamil-Canadian volunteers could speak the language and aligned quickly with community needs. Because they were from the diaspora rather than foreigners, people trusted them faster. The partner credited Kumaran's team as the secret ingredient—their cultural knowledge meant they knew how to communicate and could accomplish more in a shorter time with the Tamil stakeholders. He said, "Man, your volunteers made all the difference."

With their participation, the dynamics shifted dramatically. One partner from Sri Lanka reached out to Kumaran and expressed their appreciation. While the Australian and New Zealand volunteers did their best, it was the Canadian team's ability to speak Tamil and their innate understanding of the community that turned the situation around. They were able to complete a two-year project in six months. Kumaran noted, "The community was no longer nervous or suspicious about what the volunteers were trying to do. Third-culture kids can unlock opportunities quickly to scale ideas and businesses globally because of the soft power conferred by their multicultural breadth."

This scenario exemplifies the profound leverage and soft power that diaspora members or third-culture individuals can bring to international development projects. They can engage and move the agenda much faster because of their connection with the local culture and bridge language gaps.

With my cofounder, business partner, and friend, Kumaran Nadesan

Yesterday I was clever, so I wanted to change the world.
Today I am wise, so I am changing myself.

—RUMI

CHAPTER 4

THE EIA METHOD

I ENJOYED GROWING up in Winnipeg, Canada. It wasn't just my home. It's always been a symbol of strength to me.

My aunt (my father's eldest sister) gave me a sense of what it meant to be Canadian. She ensured that we prayed at home for our Hindu traditions and celebrated our traditional holidays like Thai Pongal and Deepavali while also celebrating Christmas and Thanksgiving. I would be learning Tamil dances one day, watching political debates the next, and then cheering on Canadian Olympic skater Brian Orser. This is where I learned what it means to be Tamil Canadian. We could keep our culture while embracing the culture around us. And we had a tremendously rich culture to enjoy.

Since 1970, Winnipeg has been hosting a beautiful event called Folklorama, which attracts thousands of people from different parts of the world. It is the largest and longest-running multicultural festival in the world, held annually for two weeks each August. Folklorama celebrates the cultural diversity of the city by inviting visitors to experience the authentic food, entertainment, and traditions of various ethnic communities by visiting pavilions set up across Winnipeg in school gyms, churches, and other venues.

Typically, there are more than forty pavilions, each representing a different culture and featuring live performances like traditional songs and dances, cultural displays, or workshops.

I was confused about my identity during my teen years, being Tamil by heritage, British by citizenship and birth, and now living in Canada with a British accent. I struggled to understand how I could be Canadian. Folklorama played a significant role in helping me realize that I wasn't alone. I saw other kids who were just as confused as I was, but had found their place as Ukrainian Canadians or Ethiopian Canadians or Japanese Canadians. It made me realize that I fit in too.

Today, whenever I feel off-kilter, I return to Winnipeg, either physically or in my imagination, and it helps me remember who I am. But I wasn't meant to stay in Winnipeg my whole life.

After I finished my undergraduate studies there in 2000, I was living my twenty-one-year-old life to the fullest. That's when my father had his first heart attack while working in Bangladesh and everything changed for me. It was an overnight transformation. One day I was doing shots with my buddies at the university bar, and the next I was stepping off a plane into this completely foreign (nonalcoholic) country. For the second time in my life, I was truly an outsider. Once again, I didn't belong.

The contrast between Winnipeg and Bangladesh was shocking. Everything was unfamiliar. I didn't know the language. I didn't know a soul there besides my father. The sights, sounds, and even smells were overwhelming. It's an understatement to say I was not prepared for how vastly different this new culture would be from what I knew.

I had a full head of thick black hair then, and with my skin tone, I looked like a local. People just expected me to understand them. But of course, I didn't understand them, and they didn't understand me when I tried to explain why. My mother tongue is Tamil and not

Bangla, which is what they speak there. Additionally, my family is Hindu, not Muslim, so I had a very different context from everyone around me.

In short, I was completely out of my comfort zone in every possible way. Regardless, I had no choice but to learn how to work in the business very quickly so that I could support my father while he recovered.

My response to all of this was to decide I didn't belong. I held tightly to everything familiar, to those few things that made me feel like me because, in my mind, those things were what defined me. I held onto the old story of my life in Canada because it was safe. Writing a new story for myself was terrifying.

Looking back now, I realize how lucky I was to have been able to learn the things I learned at that time in my life. But you would never have been able to convince me at that point how fortunate I was. I fought everything for two whole years.

Then finally, exhausted, I began to let go of the familiar and embrace the unfamiliar. That is a very scary thing to do, especially when you are a young adult who has never really experienced the "real" world. But I slowly started to really see and experience the beauty of where I was. For me, it was the people who helped me appreciate my new home. It was the friends who I connected with when I took my MBA classes. They introduced me to the beauty of the Bangladeshi culture and of their city.

At work, we would have big sales events, and people would enjoy dancing. They would play their favorite songs and hearing them continuously became familiar to me. They would bring me joy because music has a beautiful way of doing that. It's universal. You don't need to know the language to feel the rhythm.

At the end of the day, it was connecting with people and enjoying what they enjoyed, like dancing and laughing and breaking bread that softened my heart.

EIA METHOD

While I didn't suddenly discover all the answers about how to build successful business relationships, my early experiences in Bangladesh allowed me to begin to develop a three-step approach that has successfully guided me throughout my life and career. Since I first began shaping the ideas, I've shared my approach with the people I've mentored and at conferences when I am asked to speak. This method has been central to my life as a businessman, a friend, a colleague, a leader, a husband, and a father.

It's a three-step approach that I believe can guide one to flourish in diverse environments.

EIA.

Embed, Interpret, Act.

Embed: Cultural Immersion

"Embed" is based on the idea that we learn best when we have sincere connections and understanding with a new environment and the people within it. It begins with embracing the places we are in and seeing new experiences as opportunities to grow, not things to be afraid of.

Since those challenging years in Bangladesh, I have lived and traveled to many places around the world. I'm living proof that when I've embedded myself into the communities I have lived in, worked in, and visited, I've succeeded.

I think it's human nature when facing something new to resist it. For me, the initial challenge of embedding is letting go of the thought that what is familiar is best. New things represent a change from the status quo and disruption from the expected way of life. We feel out of control. Lack of predictability can create anxiety and apprehension because no matter how much we prepare, we can never truly be ready for something we haven't experienced before. It is human nature to focus more on the risk than the potential benefit of new things because our brains are wired in this way. Familiar means safe, and safe means survival.

When I immerse myself in local cultures, I gain a more compassionate lens, leading to a deeper appreciation and even love for the new place. When I opened up and began to embed myself in Bangladesh, I began acting like a part of this new culture. My social life and mental health improved along with my work attitude and performance. My new attitude made it much easier to build relationships with potential clients, leading to higher sales and more frequent closed deals.

As many expats will attest, it all starts with language. Language is not just a communication tool, it is the key to embedding and understanding. If you have ever traveled to a foreign place, you know that when you can't understand the signs and the people around you, you feel very isolated. I finally started loosening up and opening my mind to learning new words every day in Bangla from the people around me. I started watching their version of Sesame Street, a children's program called "Sisimpur." I was excited when I discovered that the national stations broadcast the news in both English and Bangla, so I would watch both versions to get a better understanding of vocabulary and the words that were relevant to my life.

As I started to try to use this new language, it took a lot of humility because I regularly got things wrong. Like most people when they learn a new language, I understood more than I could speak. I was in a position in my father's company where I was delivering a lot of training to our employees, so I had to learn words fast. I would use certain phrases during those training sessions, and if they worked, I would keep using them and then learn more. But sometimes, people would laugh when I said the wrong thing. I had to let go of my embarrassment and not worry about it.

I never became fully fluent in speaking Bangla, but my sincere efforts to try paid off massively. This is the case anywhere in the world. Language is an unbelievably powerful way to understand culture because it allows us to understand and respect people more. Through language, we can learn about the customs we see and better appreciate how in many cultures, there's a respectful way to address a person in a less formal way. This is the case in almost every language. When you embrace and embed yourself in the language, you understand when people are giving you respect and how to return that respect to them.

My wife speaks Russian, and she has taught me that it's not always what you say that matters. It's also about how you choose to say things that is critical to understanding. I know most languages have these kinds of subtle but crucial nuances.

Some languages have very specific and unique features that are important for visitors to understand if they want to fully appreciate the culture. I love the example of the extremely rare Australian Aboriginal language spoken by the Guugu Yimithirr people in Far North Queensland. One of the most distinct characteristics of this language is that it uses cardinal directions (north, south, east, west) rather than egocentric directions (left, right, front, back) for spatial orientation. Maintaining spatial awareness and direction is hugely important to their culture if you want to establish shared meaning. Infants are taught to use geographic markers from early on. Their cradles are even positioned so newborns face east to learn from birth where the sun rises. Elders teach young children to find east and west based on the positions of the sun during sunrise/sunset and note landmarks from these reference points in their desert environment.

In daily communication, rather than saying something like, "The house is left of the store," they would say, "The house is north of the store." That doesn't seem to be different from English, but let's say you were in someone's home for a meal. Instead of saying "pass the bread to your left," they would ask you to "pass the bread to the west." Even indoors, subtle geographic cues and an innate sense of orientation are key to effective communication.

If I were a business leader who wanted to bring my goods or services here, I would need to be highly conscious of this nuance so that I did not inadvertently confuse or alienate them. I would make a point to learn the cardinal directions and figure out how to tune my internal compass so that I was able to communicate more clearly. This is what it means to embed.

My good friend and the Senior Vice President of my company, Wazeer (TJ) Jalal, had an experience with this recently. He is highly educated, speaks multiple languages, and has traveled all over the world. But even so, it's easy to make cultural mistakes. When this happens, it's not the end of the world. He explained:

> I took a trip to Vietnam for our company. I wanted to understand the cultural norms there, so that I could make people comfortable. I wanted to make sure that my welcome gestures don't make people think that I'm not friendly. As Canadians, we are friendly. We are known for our hospitality. So I tried to learn how Vietnamese people behave in a meeting, the right way of shaking hands, and things like that.

I thought I had done everything right, using the correct words like "xin chào" for "hello" and expressing my gratitude for everything they said by saying "cám ơn," which means "thank you." However, the way I said it and the way it sounded to the locals in Vietnam was "câm miệng," which means "shut up" in English.

Nobody bothered to correct me because they thought it might be impolite. They all kept quiet until the last day when my cab driver finally pointed out my mistake. He said, "What you're saying is you're asking me to keep my mouth shut."

He put his finger on his lips and said, "You're asking me to do this."

So he taught me the right way of saying it, but it was too late by that time. That was a huge lesson for me. You only do business in a new country if you really are understanding the other person's culture. It's not that they've come your way. You've gone their way to do business in their country. Understanding the culture and the norms of that country, understanding their history, how they do business, all those things matter so much.

It's not just your product. It's not what you then offer them. It's not what your product can do for them. If there is no cultural fit, this business cannot happen. Experiencing that firsthand made a lot of difference. In fact, when I got back home, I sent an email apologizing for my error.

Believe it or not, they replied back saying, "I'm glad you learned." One person on a phone conversation said in a nice way, "I'm glad that you learned this. When you said it, we thought we knew what you meant, but we wished that you would've got the pronunciation correct."

At the end of the day, these are little things that make a lot of difference. Sometimes people think it's okay to take these things for granted, but no. In the real world, little things matter. The big picture only happens when you take care of those little finer details.

With Wazeer 'TJ' Jalal, Senior VP Education and Training, 369 Global

Interpret: Avoiding Misunderstanding

The second step of the method is "interpret." In our day-to-day lives, our brains are constantly receiving information. Whether it's through observation, listening, participating, reading, or through connection with others, it never stops. This information has the power to shape how we see the world and how we want to respond to it. In other words, how we see the world influences our reality. The case is magnified dramatically when we are in an unfamiliar place.

My wife Dasha has an elder sister, Yulia, who lives in Ukraine. With the ongoing war there, Yulia sent her daughter Karina to Toronto. But Karina faced significant challenges adapting to her new environment and deeply missed her home. During their conversation about this, Yulia shared some profound advice with Karina: "The place isn't going to love you until you love it back." This advice struck a chord with me, recalling my own experiences in Bangladesh.

After resisting and fighting the strange new home I was in, I eventually humbled myself and started making an earnest effort to become a part of it. I had to interpret what was happening around me to create a new perspective, and when I did, the story of who I was grew richer and more textured.

The main risk of inaccurate interpretation is that cultural mis- understandings can very easily occur, often leading to misinterpreta- tions and unintended consequences. Did you know that in different cultures, hand gestures can have varying meanings? What is acceptable in one culture may be offensive in another. The simple hand gesture for "ok" in North America seems innocuous enough. But it has wildly different meanings in other countries. In Japan, it means money or coins, and it is confusing (and even rude) to use it unless it is with both hands and in front of the body politely. In parts of Africa, it signifies the evil eye or a curse, deeply unsettling to locals there. In Brazil, it means you are indicating that someone has "zero" intelli- gence, a huge insult. And in Germany, Hungary, Russia, Greece, and France, it is obscene and offensive.

The last thing we want when trying to embed ourselves into a new culture is to inadvertently cause confusion and awkwardness. In a business context, cultural misunderstandings can arise from differences in communication styles and social norms. Varied inter-pretations of polite and respectful behavior, greetings, business card exchanges, and negotiation practices can lead to misunderstandings and affect the development of strong business relationships. For instance, the interpretation of phrases such as "sit anywhere" or "it's fine" can vary significantly between different cultures, leading to confusion and miscommunication. I once heard a story of the head of a Chinese delegation being greeted by a junior member of a US marketing team and was told to "sit where you like." The Chinese delegate left without signing a contract because he had felt humiliated due to the cultural difference in the importance of hierarchy. Had the young team member prepared ahead of time, she would have known that in a business meeting in China, it is of vital importance to show respect and courtesy. She would have addressed each of the delegates by their name and title, in order of seniority. When doing the introductions, she would have indicated where each was to sit, with the most important person being offered the seat of honor. Her team would then have ensured everyone had time to share business cards as well, according to Chinese business etiquette.

Our cultural sensitivity can make or break our chances of building relationships. I learned this the hard way during one of my first meetings with a major Bengali supplier. My father had asked me to handle an order for him, and I felt confident I could manage the task without any help. I went to this man's office to discuss the terms of the order. He invited me to sit down and have tea or coffee with him. I didn't want tea or coffee, so I declined in what I thought was a polite way and left.

The supplier didn't send the shipment he agreed to send. When my father asked the man what happened, he said it was because I had refused his offer to sit down and talk over tea. I had completely misinterpreted his invitation and acted on my wrong assumptions. I didn't realize that it wasn't about the beverage. I could have been drinking maple syrup, for all he cared. As is common in that culture, he wanted to sit down and get to know the person he was doing business with. I thought I was showing respect by not wasting his time because, from my perspective, bosses are busy people. But he interpreted it as a young man who was disrespecting and rejecting him. Because of that, he did not want to do business with me. Thankfully I was able to make contact with him, apologize, and join him for tea (water in my case) later on. He became a good friend and a guide to me from then on.

Cultural misunderstandings can, and often do, affect interpersonal and business relationships by impeding effective communication, creating unintended conflicts, and influencing consumer behavior. Understanding and respecting cultural differences is essential for building strong and successful relationships.

In my mind, all of this boils down to ethnocentrism, the belief in the superiority of one's own culture. Traditional Western thought is only one of many perspectives. Combining new information with existing information creates a whole new perspective. This is what happens when we interpret; we have a richer worldview with much more to offer.

Act: Moving Forward

To "act" means putting what you have seen, heard, and learned into practice. It involves asking questions like: How do I use my insights? What can I learn from my improved understanding? How do I need to change my behavior so I connect better with others?

As my good friend and serial entrepreneur Vern Vipul said, "Every market is different and we have to be quick to adapt and be open to learn in order to figure out that market. Leaders have to be willing to go into that place themselves. It's not something you can delegate."

As you have read already, it's important to understand that our usual approaches may not have the same impact as they do where we come from. Sometimes, we need to tweak things and create something new.

You may have heard a quote that has been attributed to Aristotle: "The whole is greater than the sum of its parts." There is a term among scientists and philosophers called "emergence" that comes into play here. The phenomenon of emergence describes how novel properties can arise in complex systems that are not inherent to their individual parts. This concept fascinates scientists and philosophers alike. Think of when ants collectively create sophisticated colonies or when solitary voices unite into transcendent choirs—emergence illuminates the irrepressible creativity of life and nature. Though we may never fully control it, emergence compels us to welcome surprise, empower autonomy, and celebrate the fathomless potential of the unexpected. Our greatest breakthroughs are often not built by design, but rather seeded when we let go of control and allow ourselves to emerge as something new and better than before.

One of the many things I've learned over the course of my life is that everyone has a story, a unique collection of connected moments that's made them who they are and how they see the world. Our stories continue to be written with every new experience and every new day. When we experience the "new," whether it's a new job, a new city, or even a new country, we're writing a new chapter in our story. Ours is a book that is waiting to be filled with stories that are waiting to be told and waiting to be read.

In my case, it wasn't until I became determined to embrace, interpret, and become comfortable with all of the unfamiliar things that changed for me in Bangladesh. I loosened up and opened myself up to my new reality. When I did that, I started seeing the beauty of the place I would call home for the next eight years. I started to really see and experience where I was. I was the same person, just in a different context. I began attending events and enjoying new foods. I even started playing cricket! It wasn't just my social life that improved, but my mental health did as well.

It wasn't easy, though. Initially, I was afraid that if I opened up and allowed myself to change, I would lose myself. How wrong I was. By being vulnerable, I lost nothing. I was the same person I had always been, but I grew into a newer, better version of myself. It was only after I let go of my fear that I began to love the new home where I would live for several years.

I have returned to Bangladesh many times since then. I have been fortunate to be able to work on producing films and TV shows that highlight the beauty of this and other cultures. At one point, I was with a film crew in the slums of Dhaka, and we heard some kids laughing and having a wonderful time nearby. We discovered them playing cricket in the middle of a garbage field. Anyone who has been to a slum knows that these garbage fields have a stench that is so strong it makes your eyes water. Yet, here they were, cheering and having a marvelous time.

We watched as one of the children hit a six, and it just went flying. Another kid ran and jumped up high to catch the ball and fell right into a soggy pile of garbage. It was absolutely disgusting.

We all sat there stunned, watching as his body completely sank, engulfed in the slurry of trash. A moment passed and we waited in silence, not realizing that we were all holding our breath. Then suddenly, as if it had been in a movie, we saw a little arm shoot straight out of the trash, triumphantly holding the ball.

Everyone went wild!

It was just incredible. It was one of those moments where you stop and realize that human nature is the same everywhere. I might have been living on the other side of the world, but these children had the same kind of joy I see on the faces of kids in my beloved Canada when playing their sport of choice—hockey.

Those moments of joy are universal. Why does this matter? Because we have so much more in common than we have differences. It is so easy to connect when you keep that in mind.

THE EIA METHOD IN ACTION

You've probably heard people say you should network and get involved in your community. It's so true! I always tell my students at Computek College that if you want to relate to folks in Toronto, go to a Toronto Maple Leafs game, or the Toronto Raptors, or the Toronto Blue Jays. You don't need language to do a high five or to cheer. Sports is one of the many great ways to connect with people.

It's not about assimilation. It's about adaptation and change for the better. It's about growth.

I love an example that Rathana Peou Norbert-Munns came up with when I was talking to her about this book. She pointed out that in our journey as global entrepreneurs, we often find ourselves anchored to the familiar—our native culture, language, and business practices. Yet, to truly thrive in a global marketplace, we must dare to venture beyond the safety of these known shores.

Think about the unique resilience of mangrove forests, comparing their roots to the experience of cultural adaptation. Unlike towering trees with roots buried deep underground, mangroves reveal a network of tangled roots above the waterline, withstanding the constant ebb and flow of tides.

Norbert-Munns said, "In this kind of journey of finding your roots, you actually need to destroy some of them in order to generate new ones."

The image of a mangrove's roots, often battered by the elements yet robust and adaptive, serves as a poignant illustration of how exposure and flexibility can foster resilience. Mangroves, with their roots exposed, invite us to consider how exposure to new environments—embracing their challenges and adapting to their rhythms—strengthens us. By allowing our roots to stretch out, vulnerable and unshielded, we encounter growth in ways we couldn't have foreseen, much like mangroves that bend but don't break against the onslaught of nature's forces.

These roots do more than simply hold the tree in place; they are dynamic, absorbing nutrients, breathing in the coastal air, and providing a haven for marine life. These remarkable trees not only withstand harsh conditions but also play a crucial role in combating climate change by sequestering large amounts of carbon in their dense wood and rich soil. Similarly, when we expose our cultural roots—when we immerse ourselves in the local language, when we sit down to share a meal, when we participate in traditional celebrations—we are not just visitors in a new land. We become a part of the living ecosystem of that culture, contributing to it as much as we draw from it.

The metaphor of the mangrove forest is a call to deeply understand before diving into action for global leaders. It suggests that we need to break out from our silos and be willing to expose and entwine our roots with those of others. Only by doing so can we grow in new directions, just as mangroves do—resilient, resourceful, and ever-reaching toward the sunlit surface.

This concept, the vulnerability coupled with the potential for powerful growth, underpins the essence of the EIA method. It illustrates the need for courage to face new challenges head-on and humility to accept that we are part of a larger, interconnected world. Rathana's insights remind us that in our global ventures, we may need to momentarily forsake the comfort of our deep-seated roots to discover new strengths and capabilities—much like the mangrove, which, through its exposure, finds its resilience—and replace kindness at the heart of those connections.

Like the intertwining of the mangrove roots, networking can be a difficult challenge. But these uncomfortable experiences are important so that we can reflect and interpret and get comfortable with using the EIA method in everyday life. For me, networking, getting involved with local initiatives, and authentically connecting with people were key to feeling at home. Doing this helped me understand more about where I was and building connections made me feel less isolated by showing me different opportunities.

I know it can be difficult to stay positive when things are frightening and unfamiliar. I also understand how it feels to want to give up when things just aren't working out the way you hoped they would. I encourage everyone who reads this to keep pushing forward and never give up. Each of us has the power to write our own story, the talent to make a change, and the opportunity to make a positive impact in any community where we find ourselves. Your unique skills, experiences, and perspectives are exceptional, and so are those of everyone else you meet.

On paper, the EIA method is a simple three-step system that offers a practical approach for engaging in diverse environments and building successful interpersonal relationships anywhere in the world. The "Embed" step emphasizes the importance of embracing new environments and being open to things that are unfamiliar. The "Interpret" step highlights the need to combine new information with existing knowledge to gain a richer perspective and to avoid cultural misunderstandings. The "Act" step focuses on putting insights into practice and being open to changing your story.

On paper, it seems like a simple and logical process that should be easy to follow. In practice, however, it takes constant conscious effort and a willingness to overcome discouragement. Determination is key. As my friend, the CEO of the Institute for Canadian Citizenship, Daniel Bernhard said about going into new markets, "We have to be open. If we shut ourselves down, we close ourselves to the lessons that we could learn from people who are already there, and we do so at our peril. We lose when that happens."

I believe that if this method is used regularly, it can unlock powerful connections around the world. The EIA method is an approach that will allow anyone to enjoy a journey of personal growth and adaptation to better understand and embrace the universal nature of human experiences.

Keep walking, though there's no place to get to. Don't try to see through the distances. That's not for human beings.

—RUMI

CHAPTER 5

FIRST GLOBAL DATA

FIRST GLOBAL DATA was founded in 2001 by Andre Itwaru, Nayeem Ali, and Manny Bettencourt. They had all worked together while at organizations like AT&T and KPMG and took the bold step to start First Global Data Inc., a company looking to innovate the money remittance sector.

"Remittance" is the term used for the process in which migrant workers send money home, a practice that plays a crucial role in supporting families and communities in many countries, particularly in developing nations where they can be a significant source of income and help reduce poverty.

In fact, remittances represent one of the largest financial inflows to developing countries, exceeding official aid and foreign direct investment in many cases. In 2022, global remittances reached a staggering $860 billion in 2023, according to the World Bank's Global Remittances Guide.[1] The same source also stated that as of 2022, the top remittance-receiving countries and amounts were India ($100 billion),

---

1   Migration Data Portal, "Remittances," https://www.migrationdataportal.org/themes/remittances.

Mexico ($60.3 billion), China ($51 billion), the Philippines ($38 billion), Egypt ($32.3 billion), and Pakistan ($29 billion).

The founders of First Global Data recognized the immense potential that lay in the facilitation of cross-border transactions, particularly for places in Latin America and the Caribbean, where a significant portion of the population worked abroad and regularly sent money back home to support their families.

I worked directly with Nayeem Ali. Nayeem is Guyanese by birth, so he was familiar with the Caribbean and Latin American markets. The founders were all third-culture kids who had lived for years in Canada, so starting this business was a natural evolution of their expertise and interests.

Back then, the idea of sending money electronically was still considered very innovative. First Global began to establish itself as a key player in the financial technology industry before the term "fintech" even really existed. First Global was a pioneer in the online remittance industry, developing a platform that allowed users to facilitate money transfer transactions through the internet, similar to the services provided by Western Union.

In this case study, I will use the story of First Global Data to examine how the company leveraged the EIA method to identify opportunities, gather new information, and navigate the challenges of expanding into new markets. The company ultimately did not succeed in the way we hoped to, but I learned that by embedding ourselves in local communities, interpreting cultural nuances, and acting upon insights gained, we were able to position the company for short-term success in the highly competitive remittance industry.

MY STORY WITH FIRST GLOBAL DATA

My father and I met the First Global Data (FGD) team around 2006. I had been working in Bangladesh for several years by then, and I was keen to get back to Canada to pursue my law degree. Plus my father had fully recovered from his heart attack in 2000 and was in full force managing the family business in Asia.

As I was preparing for my LSATs to apply for law school, I decided to pursue a financial services underwriting course at Seneca College. There were exciting things happening in the finance space in 2007, and no one was thinking of the global financial crisis which would occur a few years later.

Money markets have been a highly lucrative space for a very long time. Western Union started money transfers around 1871,[2] and internationally, money remittance was happening globally for a long time. Not necessarily always via legitimate means, but if you had someone whom you could trust, you could move money.

Since I had been working in Bangladesh, India, and Sri Lanka for a few years, I knew firsthand the potential of this industry. People from all over Asia were coming to work as laborers in countries that were keen to develop and had the money to do it. The laborers would send their money home to their families. But, if you didn't have the right person to help, you would lose the money that you worked so hard for, and trust me, if you were a laborer in that part of the world, there was nothing but hard work.

The potential of getting into this industry was huge!

My father came to Toronto to visit and, seeing my interest in the finance sector, mentioned a meeting with a group of guys who

---

2   Tom Standage, *The Victorian Internet: The Remarkable Story of the Telegraph and the Nineteenth Century's On-line Pioneers* (Pbk. ed., New York: Walker, 2007), 119. ISBN 9780802716040.

had a start-up in the remittance sector in Toronto. I was intrigued for several reasons. I was excited to attend the meeting and was keen to learn more about the industry and what FGD proposed as their competitive advantage.

Andre Itwaru was the CEO, and he fit the role well. He was a great storyteller, had a great network, and had the confidence to lead the team. Manny Bettencourt was the CFO, and he was knowledgeable, confident, and a really nice guy. Nayeem Ali was quiet. He didn't seem confident at all, and I wondered if he was even excited to attend the meeting. No offense to the others at all, but Nayeem would turn out to be my favorite. Seven years later, I would later work directly under him in 2013.

The meeting went really well. They showed us a demo of the software they had developed that would allow their customers to remit online. FGD also had licenses in several key US states, which was a huge competitive advantage since not many of the other players in the industry had them.

As a start-up, they were looking to raise capital. But they were also interested in meeting my father because they heard about the business we had established in South Asia. The FGD team knew the potential of that region and was keen to hear more from us and potentially see how we could partner. We agreed to invest a small amount and to consult in any regions where we could assist, with the understanding there would be compensation for any deals we brought to the table.

It was exciting! The market was huge, and we learned quickly that we had partnered with an innovative team. We knew we had strong contacts to build the relationships needed to scale.

Around this time, my father asked what my plans for the future were. I said I would support from Canada since I wanted to finish getting my law degree. There are many reactions a father could have to that comment. My father is a self-made man, so you can fill in the blanks. Despite that, I finished my program at Seneca Polytechnic College and completed my LSATs. It was going to be my twenty-ninth birthday on July 5, 2008.

I have to back up a couple of years to give some context to what came next. Back around 2006, before leaving Asia, I had created a full cosmetics line that I affectionately called "Sofia du Monde." I told everyone my first child would be a girl and that I would name her Sofia. This would be her inheritance. I said the same thing to my wife Dasha on our first date on November 15, 2014. We would get married in November 2015, and Sofia Saraswathy Srinarayanathas was born on June 21, 2016. That's a bit of showing off, but it's my book. Where else can I do it?

Anyway, the cosmetics line was still being manufactured in Sri Lanka in 2008. My father suggested I come see the first consignment as I had created the designs, and I could also celebrate my birthday there. We stayed at the Cinnamon Grand in Colombo, one of our favorite hotels at the time. We planned to have a birthday lunch, but when we went out to the taxi, my father began to have a massive heart attack... This was number three for him.

My father is not only my father but my mentor, my business partner, and my friend. Also, like most children, he was like Superman to me. I can't find the words to describe watching my father in that moment. He was gasping for air, grasping his chest, and his eyes were full of panic. I didn't know what to do. What do you do? We were in a cab heading for the hospital and there was insane traffic. We were about a block away from the hospital and at a standstill due to the traffic on the road.

My father got out of the car and stumbled onto the street and headed for the hospital. He would periodically bang into a car as I tried to hold him steady as we rushed forward on a life-saving mission. We staggered into the hospital where he saw a stretcher and collapsed on to it, gasping, "I'm having a heart attack." They rushed him in.

I stood there. For a long time. A very long time. A doctor came up to me and asked whether he had permission to operate. I said yes and they proceeded. My father made it through the surgery with minimal damage to his heart. I stayed with my father for a couple of weeks and then left to manage the business. When my father was ready, he headed back to Canada to rest. I didn't even get a chance to apply to law schools.

What does this have to do with FGD, you might be wondering? It's the reality of life and the reality of business. You can be excited about pursuing an opportunity, but sometimes, life has other plans for you. Nothing much happened from 2006 to 2009 in terms of our contributions to FGD. We made introductions where we could and continued to engage with the team to hear about their growth and opportunities. However, when my father was in Canada, and I was back in Asia, my father engaged with them more, and I began connecting with people who would help with expansion in Asia.

Nayeem made a plan to come to Asia, and we set up critical meetings for him to assess the market. The meetings were fruitful and, upon his return to Canada, we formalized contracts and focused on expansion in the South Asian regions.

While Nayeem was in Bangladesh, I shared some of the work we had been doing in the region. We had established businesses in Bangladesh, India, Sri Lanka, and Malaysia and continued to trade with various other countries in Asia. Our businesses ranged from manufacturing, distribution, IT, real estate, cosmetics, and consumer goods to finance, hotels, travel, farming, and agriculture. Some projects were great successes while many were epic failures, but all of them provided great insights and opportunities for learning. From the age of twenty-one to twenty-eight, I was a sponge, learning and absorbing everything I could about different industries and different markets all over the world.

In 2010, I had the opportunity to purchase a Mobile Virtual Network Operator (MVNO) in the UK called Priyo Communications. The full Priyo story comes in the next chapter, but for the purposes of the FGD story, there was a huge insight that I must share now.

As I mentioned earlier, the world of money transfers has been happening for decades. I saw transfers within rural areas of Bangladesh as well as internationally. While I was running Priyo in the UK, I also saw people in London transferring money to Bangladesh via their cell phones.

I observed street vendors and small shops selling SIM cards and facilitating money remittance through cell phones. People would give cash to the vendors, who would then text message their friends and family in the countries to arrange that the information be passed along to the correct parties who were waiting to receive the money. This was how they knew that they could go pick up their money. This was an illegal transaction. Essentially, it was money laundering because they didn't want to pay the rates to do it legally. This was not happening as an actual money transfer via SMS rather, it was a message or an image shared that confirmed something like, "I have the pounds here in London, please release the taka in Bangladesh to the receiver."

Without realizing it at the time, I happened to be embedding myself in the local marketplace where money transfers and remittance activities were taking place. I walked the streets regularly and sat in local shops drinking tea among the local people and observing the market dynamics, most specifically to observe the remittance habits of the local London Bangladeshi expat community.

In a way, this informal system functioned akin to a courier service for cash; it was decentralized, community-driven, and operated on a foundation of personal connections, allowing it to bypass traditional financial institutions' complexities and fees. I shared my insights with Nayeem.

I wish I could take credit for what happened next, but I can't. However, my insights did validate a project that the FGD team was working on—mobile remittance.

FGD was early in the web-based remittance space. Now, they were also one of the first to be able to facilitate mobile remittance. With the licenses they had in the US, the innovative technology they developed, and the global customer base they had built, they went public on November 30, 2012.

After exiting Priyo Communications unhappily (again more on this later), I happily went back to Canada to join Nayeem and the team as Director of International Business Development at FGD in 2013.

Since I knew the founders well, especially Nayeem, and had been involved early on in the global expansion, my role was to nurture the current markets and the market partners we had established while also researching and establishing new markets. After years of global entrepreneurship, I was sitting in an office in Toronto doing a 9:00 a.m. to 5:00 p.m. job.

How did I feel? Wonderful at first. I was looking forward to getting back to Canada and excited to be in Toronto. I had invested in a few pre-construction condos in 2004, and by 2013, I could move into one right downtown. I was single in a city I loved, taking on an exciting role with a company I knew as a start-up that just went public!

I reported directly to Nayeem, and he was a great boss. I learned so much from him, and he took me under his wing to show me the ropes of business in Toronto. He was always looking for opportunities to learn more, to enter markets, to expand the business, and to increase revenue. He always brought me into his meetings which gave me insights into how to conduct them and handle the presentations, but more importantly, I watched how he worked the room.

We had a meeting to attend in Washington D.C., and I was excited to join him on the trip. When we got to the airport and headed to immigration, Nayeem was held for further questioning. As a publicly listed company in the remittance industry with US licenses, we were audited and heavily regulated. In fact, we had regular check-ins with the FBI, Royal Canadian Mounted Police (RCMP), and other organizations to ensure we adhered to regulations, and we were careful to avoid suspicion of any money laundering activity. When Nayeem was held at the border, I knew it wasn't for any other reason other than his name. Nayeem Ali, like most Muslim names, were red flags due to the tragedy on 9/11.

I called Manny to let him know what happened. Manny told me to get on the plane and close the deal. Once I arrived in D.C., Nayeem was able to get on a later flight and met me in time for the meeting.

It was interesting. We were connecting with a group of gentlemen who were interested in promoting the FGD remittance products through their vast network across the US. At one point in the meeting, Nayeem had to step away to take a call. One of the guys asked me where I was from. I shared my history in as brief a manner as possible. He said, "Oh, you're from Europe. That's why your pants are so skinny."

I looked at their suits and saw they were all wearing Zoot suits. You never know what world you're going to step into or how you're going to be judged.

My role at FGD was wonderful, and Nayeem was an amazing boss. But the one thing that bothered me was control. After being an entrepreneur most of my life, I didn't have the ability to set the direction of the organization. It didn't matter whether Nayeem was right or wrong in his decision-making. He was making decisions from a vantage point and responsibility that I didn't have. I wanted to be in that seat, especially since most of my life I had been the one to call the shots. This became very clear to me when the topic of bitcoin came around.

Bitcoin is the first decentralized cryptocurrency. It operates on a peer-to-peer network, allowing for secure and anonymous transactions without the need for a central authority like a bank or government. Introduced in 2009, bitcoin is the first and most well-known cryptocurrency and has gained significant traction as an alternative to traditional currencies. This has consistently attracted investors, merchants, and individuals seeking a decentralized and transparent financial system.

I was intrigued by the emerging developments in what would be later called the "fintech" space, particularly in the areas of money remittance and cryptocurrencies. As the company was already well-established in the industry by the time I came into the picture, I saw an opportunity to explore these new frontiers and learn more about their potential impact on global finance.

Around 2012–2013, I began to delve deeper into the world of cryptocurrencies, and I was fascinated by the possibilities. I remember stumbling upon a bitcoin ATM near our offices on Spadina Avenue in Toronto and later found out that it was operated by Anthony di Lori who would go on to become one of the co-founders of Ethereum, a groundbreaking platform which is currently positioned second to bitcoin.

I believed FGD should take a lead in this up-and-coming sector. An opportunity presented itself when a group of entrepreneurs approached us with an idea to set up a cryptocurrency exchange platform called Butter Coin. They were interested in partnering with First Global Data to offer remittance services and other financial products and, stating the obvious, they needed to connect with FGD to gain access to the remittance licenses FGD held. On March 28, 2013, the market capitalization of bitcoin reached 1 billion USD. On April 1, 2013, the exchange rate for 1 bitcoin (BTC) was 100 USD. An April Fools' joke to some perhaps but, as I write this in 2024, the current valuation of bitcoin is around 64,000 USD.

I naively believed that venturing into the cryptocurrency space could be a promising opportunity for the company. We arranged a meeting with the Butter Coin team to discuss the potential partnership. I have to thank and credit Nayeem for taking the meeting and encouraging me. While the concept was interesting, we quickly realized that navigating the regulatory landscape would be a significant hurdle. Ultimately, the idea fell through due to the complexity of obtaining regulatory approvals.

Later, when I pursued my Masters of Law at the University of Toronto, I focused my research on blockchain technology and bitcoin. I discovered that many of my professors and peers viewed cryptocurrencies as an illegal, underground system of transactions. At the time, there were indeed many bad actors in the space, particularly in the drug industry, who exploited the lack of regulation for illicit activities.

However, I remained convinced that the underlying concept and infrastructure of cryptocurrencies held immense potential, much like the early days of the internet in the 2000s. Just as the internet attracted both good and bad players, I believed that the cryptocurrency space needed the involvement of ethical, responsible individuals and organizations to establish proper structures and ensure that the technology could benefit society as a whole.

Fast forward to 2024, and we see that major financial institutions are now seriously exploring bitcoin and other cryptocurrencies. While there is still a long way to go in terms of establishing a robust regulatory framework, the industry has made significant strides in legitimizing itself.

In my current role, I am a sponsor and active participant in an organization called Blockchain North, which aims to promote good players in the Web 3.0 space. I remain on the lookout for opportunities in the sector, as I firmly believe that it will continue to be a strong and influential industry in the years to come.

As I said, I believe Nayeem made the right decision for the company. With the regulatory scrutiny FGD faced, it would jeopardize the organization and now that it was a publicly traded company, entering into the crypto space would have been a massive risk.

When I met Nayeem a couple of years ago, he had left FGD. The company had not done well for several reasons and eventually was delisted. What industry did Nayeem get into after leaving FGD? The Web 3.0 industry, specifically blockchain and cryptocurrency.

What would I have done in Nayeem's place? Would I have done anything differently? Who knows. But the event encouraged me to get back to my passion—politics! Wait, what? More on this later.

EMBED–INTERPRET–ACT: KEY INSIGHTS

First Global Data's Global Expansion

To truly understand the intricacies of the remittance industry and identify opportunities for growth, the original founders of First Global

Data recognized the importance of immersing themselves in the local markets they sought to serve. This process of embedding involved more than just surface-level research; it required a deep dive into the cultural, social, and economic factors that shape the way people send and receive money across borders.

Team dynamics play a significant role in the success of any organization. The story of FGD is no different. Teams start with leadership. The three founders at FGD—Andrea, Nayeem, and Manny—had the benefit of working together in their corporate roles which allowed them to see how each other worked. Each founder had a different personality and working style, but they complimented each other and made the partnership work. Of course, the other key factor was their third-culture perspective. Andre and Nayeem were born in Guyana and had grown up in Canada which gave them perspective on immigrant culture and the desire to send money back home to their families.

Great teams are important as is entering the right market. The remittance industry, although it had been around for decades, was entering a new phase of innovation as the sector was capitalizing on the internet. Security and safety were pain points of the current market and the internet helped to address those concerns. FGD entering the remittance industry with a new innovative way of doing things helped them capture the market quickly.

FGD made a significant acquisition of remittance companies in the Caribbean and Latin American markets in the US. As Andre and Nayeem were both from Guyana, they had experience with the Caribbean market. Acquiring a team that was already operating as a remittance company in those markets added to their strengths.

The Latin American market was a new, but a massive, market to step into and scale. FGD ensured they regularly visited the offices across the US with a significant focus on Texas and Florida, as these states had the largest volumes at the time. The team FGD built had experience in the Latin American market, but the FGD leadership needed to understand the market and it was wise of them to make frequent visits to embed themselves in the culture. A significant step was also to empower the local teams, not only because of their corporate talents but also—and perhaps more importantly—their unique cultural understanding of local markets. A global business needs to have a local understanding of the markets to succeed.

Asian Markets

On behalf of FGD, Nayeem made an important move to explore Asia. This began his process, and in turn FGD's process, of research-ing, building contacts, and establishing trade links in Asia to ensure successful expansion. In this case, Nayeem leveraged the contacts my father and I had in the region and also looked for our guidance for the nuances of doing business in Asia.

He understood that the key to success in the remittance industry lay in building strong relationships with local banks and telecom companies in other countries. By partnering with us, Nayeem knew we could complement their technology platform with our local knowledge to facilitate more seamless money transfers and provide more value to customers.

As we reflected on that exciting time, he said:

Before we even started to do business in Asia, I actually made a trip myself to Bangladesh to set up operations. We embedded ourselves there by meeting with the Deputy Governor of the Central Bank in Bangladesh and then having meetings with all the banks across Bangladesh to show them more technology.

Muraly and his father arranged these meetings for us to accommodate building those relationships. We had to understand what the landscape was and what the regulations would allow us to do and not allow us to do.

Once we understood all of those things, we were able to come back to Canada and put the agreements in place. And then we moved into Malaysia and a few other countries, which went well because we had Muraly and his father there. They understood and knew the environment really well, much better than I did obviously. I left it to them to establish that infrastructure because they were there before me.

Ensuring they understood the local markets so they could expand globally was the key reason FGD connected with my father and me. By connecting with us, FGD was able to get the insights and introductions they needed to enter the markets effectively. Not all relationships were created from the introductions my father and I made, including one of their critical connections with the software development company F1Soft; however, the insights they gained by embedding in the local culture helped FGD understand the opportunity they had in front of them with F1Soft.

This occurred in the early to mid-2000s when many companies were not looking at outsourcing their technology to parts of Asia. However, because Nayeem came to Bangladesh and saw the things that we and others were doing, he recognized an opportunity to get low-cost software that would be a game-changer for their business.

This is a critical example of the EIA method. Nayeem embedded himself in Asian culture, interpreted the opportunities he saw in the

West, and was open to what they were doing in the East. By merging Eastern technologies and talent with Western ideas, they were able to go public.

INTERPRETING CULTURAL NUANCES

To truly capitalize on the opportunities identified through this process, businesses must also develop a keen understanding of the cultural nuances that shape consumer behavior and market dynamics. This is where the second example of the EIA method with FGD comes into play.

For First Global Data, interpreting cultural nuances was not just a matter of academic interest but a critical factor in the company's ability to tailor its services to meet the unique needs of each market. By delving deeper into the cultural, social, and economic factors that influenced the way people sent and received money across borders, the company was able to identify key insights that informed its strategy and decision-making process.

As I walked the streets in London and embedded myself in the local culture and watched those street vendors and small shops facilitate money transfers through cell phones, I began to understand the intricate web of cultural, social, and economic factors that shaped these transactions. I learned why these vendors and shops were not only selling SIM cards but also facilitating money remittances through cell phones. For many Bangladeshi immigrants in the UK, sending money back home was not just a financial transaction but a deeply personal and cultural one. It was a way to support their families, maintain ties to their homeland, and fulfill their obligations as breadwinners.

By embedding myself in the local community and observing these transactions firsthand, I was able to provide these valuable insights to Nayeem, who was chief strategy officer (CSO) at the time and contributed enormously to the company's decision-making process.

But interpreting cultural nuances is not always a straightforward process. It requires an eagerness to listen, learn, and adapt to the unique circumstances of each market. It also requires a deep respect for the cultural traditions and values that shape consumer behavior and market dynamics.

In the case of FGD, this meant going beyond surface-level observations and engaging with the local community on a more intimate level. As we interpreted cultural nuances, we were able to identify key insights that informed its strategy.

The observations I made in London led to a pivotal moment for both me and FGD. It validated the company's strategy to focus on the local market and helped strengthen our ability to shape our services to meet the specific needs of this community. We began seeking ways to build more trust with our customers as we aimed to serve a greater part of the mobile remittance market.

Acting on my local insights meant making bold moves to position the company for success in the remittance industry. Nayeem Ali was always a strategic thinker, so he saw the potential there. This was the game-changer, leading us to go public in 2012.

Another key insight that emerged from this process was the importance of trust in the remittance industry. In many of the markets that FGD served, there was a deep-seated mistrust of traditional financial institutions and a preference for informal channels of money transfer. We learned that by building trust with customers through a commitment to transparency, reliability, and cultural sensitivity, we would have a better chance of overcoming this barrier and establishing ourselves as a trusted player in the industry.

The number of users on a platform dramatically increases when you offer your products and services in highly populated emerging markets—especially the remittance markets. They would ask their friends and family in other countries, "Please use this platform to send me money."

It was a huge, free marketing base.

Emerging markets also leapfrogged into the mobile phone industry. This was significant because, in most of the West, the adoption of mobile solutions was very slow. Having licenses in the West and leveraging global markets allowed FGD to capture the space quickly.

Embedding in local markets is not a one-time event but rather an ongoing process of learning and observation. By immersing themselves in the communities they serve, businesses can gain a deeper understanding of the cultural, social, and economic factors that shape consumer behavior and identify ways to improve and grow.

For businesses seeking to expand into new markets and navigate the complexities of the global marketplace, interpreting cultural nuances is a critical skill that cannot be overlooked. By appreciating the cultural, social, and economic factors that shape consumer behavior and market dynamics, entrepreneurs and business leaders can similarly identify new growth opportunities, tailor their services to meet the unique needs of each market and build trust with their target customers.

ACTING ON LOCAL INSIGHTS

Simply interpreting cultural nuances and identifying opportunities is not enough. To truly succeed in the global marketplace, businesses must also be willing to act on the insights they have gained and adapt their strategies accordingly. This is where the third component of the EIA method comes into play: Acting.

One of the most significant of these moves by FGD was the tactical acquisition of a company with remittance licenses in key US states like New York and Florida. By acquiring these licenses, FGD was able to expand its reach and tap into new markets, while also positioning itself as a major player in the industry.

But acquiring licenses was just one part of the equation. To truly succeed in these new markets, First Global also needed to plan our services to meet the unique needs of each community. This meant taking the insights gained through the process of interpreting cultural nuances and translating them into tangible actions that would benefit the company's customers. In many of the markets that we served, there were no clear roadmaps for success. We had to navigate uncharted territory and adjust to changing circumstances on the fly.

Acting on local insights is more than just developing new products and services. It's also about building relationships. At First Global, we invested heavily in local talent and expertise. We hired local staff who understood the cultural nuances of each market and could help navigate the complex web of business practices and regulations. By building a team of local experts, we were able to identify new opportunities for growth and build trust with our partners and customers.

As Nayeem said, "In my career, I have established relationships in Europe, Asia, Africa, and we are now launching all our technologies globally. Nothing has changed. It is the same mantra. Make sure you have the right talent. People are on the ground in those parts of the world who are embedded, and who understand the environment."

Our success in the immigrant market was proof of the power of acting on local insights and adapting to the unique needs of each community. For businesses seeking to succeed in the global marketplace, acting on local insights is a critical skill that cannot be overlooked.

THE IMPACT OF THE EIA METHOD

The story of First Global Data is evidence of the impact of the EIA method in action. By embedding ourselves in local markets, interpreting cultural nuances, and acting on local insights, we were able to navigate the complexities of the global marketplace and establish ourselves as a major player for at least a brief time in the remittance industry.

The impact of the EIA method goes far beyond the success of a single company. It represents a fundamental shift in the way businesses approach global expansion and cross-cultural engagement. By prioritizing local knowledge and cultural sensitivity, the EIA method challenges traditional notions of globalization and offers a new paradigm for success in the global marketplace.

One of the most significant impacts of the EIA method is its ability to build trust and credibility with local communities. By embedding ourselves in local markets and engaging with customers and partners on a deep level, we were able to gain this precious and fragile trust. This was essential to our success, particularly in this market with its deep-seated mistrust of banks and financial services.

The EIA method can drive innovation and adaptability, two essential factors in any company's success, particularly in markets where traditional business models and approaches were not well-suited to local needs.

I grew so much as an entrepreneur and as a leader during this time. From 2006 to 2013, I consulted with FGD and then became their head of international business development, getting paid in shares. I didn't stay with them long after accepting that position.

I'm an entrepreneur, through and through. I hated my role for many reasons, most particularly that I wasn't the decision-maker. People would come into the office at 9:00, leave at 5:00. On September 5, 2014, I left FGD to buy Computek College.

After I left, I slowly had to sell shares to support my other business ventures, but I got so much more than money from my time with them. All three founders, Nayeem Ali, Andre Itwaru, and Manny Bettencourt were amazing mentors and gave me great advice. I learned how important it is to have relationships with stakeholders inside and outside of your company.

Every wise leader knows that building trust is not just about establishing credibility with customers. By investing in local talent and expertise, we were able to deepen our credibility within local communities and supplement our observations by listening to what our people told us they were experiencing on the street.

Perhaps, the most significant impact of the EIA method is its ability to drive long-term, sustainable growth. By prioritizing local knowledge and cultural sensitivity, businesses that adopt it can build strong, lasting relationships with their customers and partners. These relationships are essential to long-term success in the global marketplace, where trust and credibility are often more valuable than short-term gains.

The impact of the EIA method can be seen not only in the success of First Global Data but also in the broader landscape of global business. As more and more companies seek to expand into new markets and navigate the complexities of the worldwide marketplace, the EIA method offers a road map for success that prioritizes local knowledge, cultural sensitivity, and adaptability.

Although First Global Data ultimately didn't last, the experience was beneficial for me in many ways, including providing the funds

I used to acquire Computek College. I bought Priyo before FGD went public. It's important to share both successes and losses in the entrepreneurial journey.

For me, the impact of the EIA method at this time in my life was profound, even though I didn't know that was what I had been doing. My firsthand insights and experiences have shaped my approach to business and leadership and have reinforced my belief in the importance of cultural sensitivity and local engagement. As more and more businesses embrace this approach, we have the opportunity to create a more inclusive, equitable, and sustainable global marketplace that benefits all stakeholders.

But the impact of the EIA method is not limited to the business world. It has the potential to drive positive change in communities around the world by fostering cross-cultural understanding, building bridges between diverse populations, and creating new opportunities for growth and development.

Patience with
small details makes
perfect a large work,
like the universe.

—RUMI

CHAPTER 6

PRIYO

THE STORY OF Priyo Communications, an MVNO in the UK, is another example that I like to share when I teach the EIA method. It was a time when I came to really appreciate how to navigate the complexities of going into a new market, ultimately shaping the approach to international business and cross-cultural management that I use today.

As a young entrepreneur in 2010, I had the opportunity to acquire Priyo Communications from its founder, Abdullah Ferdous. Ferdous was someone I had previously worked with to create secure, hologram-embedded certificates for my family's business in Bangladesh. He had started Priyo in the UK but struggled to capture the market and was facing bankruptcy. Recognizing the potential in the business, I saw this as an exciting opportunity to reenter the Western market. I had seen how everyone was trying to do "Western" things in this Western marketplace, and I could see the great value in doing things with a more Eastern approach there.

Mr. Faisal Alim was the chairman of the board of a major tech firm in Bangladesh called Wintel Ltd. It also turned out that he was a dear friend of my father and became a mentor and guide for me during my time there. He and I worked together on a few projects, and I quickly realized that he was on the cutting edge of the new the tech industry. It was Mr. Faisal who first alerted me to the opportunity with Priyo Mobile in the UK.

With Mr. Faisal Alim, Chairman, Wintel Ltd.; UK, 2011

With Uncle Thiru Prabhakaran (R of Muraly) and Faisal Alim (L of Muraly)

I was the managing director, and the CEO was my uncle Thiru Prabhakaran. I call him "Uncle," which is appropriate in my culture, even though he is a distant relative who I met during my time working with my father in Bangladesh. Once I knew that I was going to buy the company, I needed somebody who understood that UK space, and my uncle lived there. Even though I was born in London, I had only lived there until I was seven. I invited my uncle to join us and handle operations as the CEO. Initially, I did not plan to live in London. I went back and forth between there and Bangladesh and other countries where we were doing business, such as Malaysia and India. He was my trusted person who was embedded in the culture.

Little did I know that this acquisition would not only expand my understanding of the UK's mobile telecommunications market but also teach me invaluable lessons about the importance of local market insights and the power of the EIA method in driving business success.

In this case study, I share my journey with Priyo Communications (which overlapped with FGD) to show how I used the same experiences that I shared in the last case study to further my understanding of what I eventually came to call the EIA method.

EMBEDDING IN THE COMMUNITY

Excited by the prospect of reviving Priyo Communications, I first stepped into the role of managing director with the determination to understand the intricacies of the UK mobile phone market. What I quickly realized was that the key to our success lay not in boardroom strategizing but in the bustling streets of London, where our target customers lived and worked.

Armed with eager curiosity and driven by panic and doubt about what to do with this new company I was now responsible for, I found myself walking around town a lot to relieve stress. Without knowing it, those walks were the way I began to embed myself in the local culture. I spent countless hours wandering the streets, observing people's behaviors, and engaging in conversations with shop owners and street vendors. This grassroots approach allowed me to witness firsthand the challenges and preferences of our potential customers, many of whom were immigrants from diverse backgrounds.

The MVNO business model involved purchasing bulk minutes from established network operators and reselling them under our own brand, which presented unique challenges. We were competing against industry giants who had the resources to offer free SIM cards and aggressive pricing. On top of all that, Priyo was struggling to recover from near-bankruptcy, making it difficult for us to match these offers.

The process of embedding in the UK market was also not without its challenges. As a newcomer to the industry and the country, I had to navigate cultural differences, build relationships with key stakeholders, and earn the trust of our target customers. However, the time and effort I invested in understanding the local landscape would prove instrumental in Priyo's eventual success.

As I immersed myself in the local market, I began to notice patterns that would begin to reshape our business strategy. The key insight came when I began to associate with the local immigrant communities and saw many of them carrying two mobile phones at all times—one for local calls and another for international communication.

By embedding myself in the local culture and observing consumer behavior at a granular level, I gained invaluable insights that would later inform our product offerings and marketing approach. Through this immersive experience, I learned that true market intelligence comes not from behind a desk but from the streets and shops where real people live and work.

INTERPRETING CULTURAL NUANCES

As I interpreted the two-phone phenomenon, I found it odd and awkward that everyone carried two phones everywhere and had to keep track of two numbers. I wanted to know why they did it. I continued to embed myself in the local market and made friends with people who were doing this. One of the most significant observations I made was the importance of convenience for our target customers. They were also very savvy about looking for the best deals to help with affordability.

But this wasn't all. The prevalence of carrying two phones among Asian immigrants was not merely a matter of convenience; it was deeply rooted in their cultural values and social norms. In many Asian cultures, having multiple phones was a symbol of status and prestige, signifying a person's importance and business role. This insight helped me understand the psychological and emotional factors that influenced our customers' purchasing decisions.

Even so, the cost of maintaining two phones was a significant burden for many of them, and I learned they often had to make sacrifices to afford the high international calling rates. This presented an opportunity for Priyo to differentiate itself, which would come in the Act phase of our journey as a new business.

Interpreting this pattern also shed light on the importance of word-of-mouth marketing in immigrant communities. These close-knit networks relied heavily on personal recommendations and trusted the opinions of their peers when making purchasing decisions. This insight emphasized the need for a grassroots approach to marketing, focusing on building relationships and trust within the communities we served.

Another critical aspect of interpreting cultural nuances was understanding the role of small businesses and street vendors in the lives of our target customers. These local establishments served as community hubs, providing not only products and services but also a sense of belonging and connection to their home countries.

Interpreting cultural nuances also required a deep understanding of the diverse immigrant communities in the UK, each with their unique language, customs, and communication preferences. This knowledge was essential in developing targeted marketing campaigns and customer support services that resonated with our audience. It helped that I spoke and understood English, Tamil, Bangla, Urdu, and Hindi—some just enough to get a sense of how people responded to the purchases they were making. Of course, you don't have to be fluent in foreign languages to get a sense of universal reactions of happiness, dissatisfaction, or anger. But it did help that I understood many of the cultural nuances that I saw.

For example, I knew rejection is a practice that many cultures use as a regular part of the marketplace. You will see people in other countries reject an offer on purpose to be polite. You have to ask again and again before they accept the invitation. I knew to stay put when a rejection happened and to watch what was happening. Western observers might see the first "no" and figure that was that. But because I had experienced these cultures, I knew to wait for the third, fourth, or fifth "no" until the "yes" came.

Another observation I made came when I started to talk to the salespeople on the streets and in the shops. Meeting the vendors was so important. I saw how their choices were often made out of convenience. Shop owners had a choice to sell rice, for example. But when they did, they had to carry the large, heavy bags and find a place to store them on their shelves. When those bags were sold, they might make £1 (1 USD) profit, which isn't much for all that labor. Or, they could make a £2 profit on a tiny SIM card. In sales, you always want the easiest sale for a maximum profit. It wasn't hard to understand that there was a willing salesforce for our little SIM cards that had not really been tapped into.

The other thing I noticed was that vendors found selling boring because in the UK there was no negotiation. That's the fun part for someone from another culture. If they could chat about the SIM card and talk about what was happening in the market that was appealing. They could tell the story of how they met me, this kid from Sri Lanka who came over last month from Bangladesh. Stories are part of sales too, and they took the place of the haggling that they missed.

As I explored the cultural fabric of our target market, I realized that our success depended not only on offering competitive products and prices but also on demonstrating a genuine understanding and appreciation of the values and lifestyles of our customers and vendors. By interpreting the cultural nuances that shaped their behavior, we set ourselves up for success to build a brand that truly resonated with their needs and aspirations.

ACTING ON LOCAL INSIGHTS

Armed with a deep understanding of the local market and the cultural nuances that shaped consumer behavior, we set out to act on these insights and transform Priyo Communications into a thriving business. After Embedding and Interpreting, we were able to come up with a plan that would differentiate ourselves in three ways: (1) the local rates, (2) smaller markets, and (3) data rates.

First, we focused on offering a convenient, cost-effective solution that would eliminate the need for multiple devices as a solution to

the inconvenience of purchasing and carrying two phones. We introduced competitive pricing for local and international calls, ensuring
that our rates were on par with, or even lower than, those of our
competitors. This approach not only made our services more affordable for our customers, but it also eliminated the need for them to
carry multiple devices.

If you'll indulge me, I'd like to get a little technical for this
example because the insights I gained from embedding myself in the
industry taught me lessons that I was able to draw from for the rest
of my career. Initially, I learned that the big operators would charge
consumers £1 per minute for overseas calls (or whatever amount they
felt like charging at any given time). Because they were buying from
the big operators, the MVNOs would charge, for example, £1.50
per minute for those same calls, even though they were buying those
minutes much cheaper than £1. Why they did that, I have no idea.
But because they did, people would carry a local phone so they would
only be charged £1 a minute locally. Then, they would have their
long-distance phone because the big operators wouldn't have cheap
international rates, but the MVNOs would. To me, it made no sense
other than greed.

So, for Priyo to be competitive, the first step was that instead
of charging £1.50 for local calls like all the other MVNOs did, we
charged £1 so we could go to the customer and ask them why they were
carrying two phones. Our pitch was basically, "We're also charging
£1, so you don't need two phones anymore. We have affordable local
rates AND affordable international rates."

To further differentiate ourselves in the market, we focused on
underserved immigrant communities, such as those from the Philippines, Nepal, and Nigeria. By targeting these niche markets, we
were able to establish a strong foothold and build a loyal customer

base without engaging in direct price competition with larger, more established players.

I learned even more about the playing field and the big companies as players. Player 1 would charge something like 5 pence per minute. Player 2 would then charge 3 pence. Player 3 would charge 2 pence. So, Player 1 would then undercut that. They would fight like this, and so their rates were constantly changing.

India is a massive market, so everyone was fighting for that space. We went into India, but unlike the other MVNOs, we offered the same rates that we always offered and didn't bother to keep up with the fluctuations of the big players. We didn't care if we weren't competitive because we planned to capture smaller markets with higher success. These were the neglected places that had few options. We went into countries like Nepal, and as we had anticipated, we didn't have to fight with many competitors. Essentially, we were the big fish in the small pond.

The final differentiator was in the data rates. When we purchased Priyo, there were only two hundred customers who paid £10 a month for their call rates and data packages. Whenever they ran out of data, they had to go back to the vendor for a "top up" card. We realized that the key was the way we handled data. That became another major differentiator.

The so-called "innovative West" at the time really had no idea about the future of mobile technology. Everyone was focused on these outdated call rates and was still talking about landlines.

Remember, this is 2010. In the emerging markets of other countries, everyone had already jumped into mobile technology. The consumers were largely experienced in mobile innovation, so they were not calling on landline phones the way Western consumers still were. In these places, they're calling through Skype and Viber, which were huge at that time.

I started to wonder why we would even bother to look at trying to make money in this space where people are fighting each other over what would soon be antiquated technology?

I knew data was the future, so the answer was simple. We doubled our price on data because our target market was using so much of it. And they happily paid double because there was value in having that data available. It made sense to our customers. They figured they were saving because they didn't have to pay the high call rates.

I knew it was a risk. If there were a million people in a country, maybe ten thousand people were using data as their primary mode of communication. But we continued to focus on that smaller group of people because we were willing to hedge our bets that the insights we had gained from learning the marketplace would prove true.

We were able to establish a strong foothold and build a loyal customer base without engaging in direct price competition with larger, more established players.

A key factor in our success was my uncle Prabhakaran's understanding of the vendor networks. As a Sri Lankan Tamil, he was well-versed in the complex dynamics of the MVNO market, which was dominated by companies like Lyca and Lebara who were leaders in the space. There were many companies in this market that had grown rapidly by purchasing bulk minutes from operators and packaging them as their own mobile services. However, their business practices were sometimes questionable and even unethical at times, leading to lengthy legal battles. We had to work hard to distinguish ourselves and earn a reputation for being different than them.

It was a tough market. In the street-level business environment, having someone like my uncle who could navigate the challenges was crucial. We invested in building strong relationships with local business owners and community leaders. We recognized that these individuals played a crucial role in shaping the opinions and preferences of their communities, and by earning their trust and support, we were able to tap into powerful word-of-mouth marketing channels.

To incentivize these local partners, we introduced a commission-based system that rewarded them for every customer they brought on board. We also provided them with marketing materials and training to help them effectively promote our services within their communities. This approach not only helped us expand our reach but also fostered a sense of ownership and loyalty among our partners.

Uncle Prabhakaran managed our sales team and dealt with the day-to-day issues that arose as well, which was crucial when problems came up. For example, when one of our salespeople was allegedly kidnapped and held for ransom, my uncle was able to assess the situation and advise against paying the ransom, as it could have been a scam orchestrated by the salesperson himself. This was the kind of environment that we operated in there in London, and his advice as someone embedded in the community saved us from making a costly error. In the end, the threat evaporated, so it was likely just what Uncle had said—a scam.

As we acted on these local insights, we began to see a significant uptick in our customer base. In less than two years, we grew from a mere 200 inactive users to over 65,000 active subscribers. This rapid growth was a testament to the power of the EIA method and the importance of tailoring our approach to the specific needs and preferences of our target market.

The success of Priyo Communications in the UK market demonstrated the immense potential of the EIA method in driving business growth and success. By embedding ourselves in the local culture, interpreting the nuances that shaped consumer behavior, and acting on these insights, we were able to transform a struggling company into a thriving enterprise.

CHALLENGES AND LESSONS LEARNED

As with all business, success was not without its challenges. As our customer base grew, so did the demand on our infrastructure and customer support services. We had to quickly adapt and scale our operations to meet the needs of our expanding user base, while also ensuring that we maintained the high level of service that our customers had come to expect.

Despite these challenges, our commitment to acting on local insights remained firm. We continued to engage with our customers, gather feedback, and refine our approach based on their evolving needs and preferences. This iterative process allowed us to stay ahead of the curve and maintain our competitive edge in a rapidly changing market.

One of the most significant challenges we faced was navigating the complex political landscape in Bangladesh, where our parent company was based. As Bangladesh underwent a major political shift, with a new party coming into power, we found ourselves in a precarious position. This sudden change in the political climate severely impacted our ability to fund our UK operations and threatened the very existence of Priyo Communications.

Faced with this unexpected challenge, I had to make difficult decisions to keep the company afloat. I explored various avenues for funding, including reaching out to potential investors and renegotiating our contracts with suppliers. However, despite my best efforts, we were unable to secure the necessary resources to sustain our growth trajectory.

I must admit that I didn't fully grasp the importance of long-term thinking and relationship building at the time. I jumped ship, so to speak. While we had successfully scaled the business and learned that we could merge Eastern and Western approaches to make a significant amount of money, I wasn't as mature as I am now as a business leader.

This experience taught me a valuable lesson about the importance of adaptability and resilience in the face of adversity. As entrepreneurs, we must be prepared to navigate unexpected challenges and make tough decisions to protect our businesses and our people.

Another key lesson I learned from my time at Priyo was the importance of long-term thinking and relationship building. In the fast-paced world of business, it can be tempting to focus solely on short-term gains and quick wins. However, my experience in the UK market taught me that lasting success comes from cultivating strong, mutually beneficial relationships with our customers, partners, and stakeholders.

This realization underscored the need for entrepreneurs to adapt their strategies and approaches to the specific cultural and institutional contexts in which they operate. By understanding and navigating these differences, we can position ourselves for success in diverse markets and build truly global enterprises.

Looking back, my time with Priyo Communications is bittersweet. These experiences are part of the entrepreneurial journey, and it's crucial to learn from them. I am grateful for the lessons learned and the insights I gained. While the journey was not without its challenges, it ultimately shaped my approach to international business and cross-cultural management, paving the way for future successes.

Let go of your mind and then be mindful. Close your ears and listen.

–RUMI

CHAPTER 7

COMPUTEK COLLEGE

I AM CURRENTLY the owner and CEO of Computek College. I purchased the college on September 5, 2014, and by 2024, we 10× our valuation. It's a business led by an immigrant, with an immigrant team that serves immigrants. Here's a glimpse into our story, and how we do what we do, with a little background on how I came to be where I am today.

In 2014, I was director of international business development at First Global Data Inc., as mentioned previously. I loved my role in this remittance fintech space, and I loved my boss Nayeem Ali, who was one of the founders and served as the CSO, but I missed the autonomy of making my own decisions. So, in May 2014, I ran to become a member of Canadian parliament in a federal by-election for the Liberal party nomination in what would later become the Trudeau government.

After living and working overseas for so long, I was eager to find an opportunity to give back to the country that had given so much to me. When Jim Karygiannis resigned, it forced a by-election for his riding, a geographic area also known as an electoral district. I was looking for a new way to contribute to Canada and believed this was an excellent way to get into politics. After speaking to my family and Nayeem, my boss, I put in my application to run and began knocking on doors.

It was eye-opening to meet people from all over the world. I was running in an area called Scarborough–Agincourt in Toronto, which had many recent and well-established immigrants. The riding also had Canadians who had been there for generations. This was completely different from the Winnipeg life I grew up in. Adding to the experience was the fact that I had lived in many of the places these immigrants were from, and I could share in some of the stories of their homeland because I had also lived there.

I heard many stories about the struggles they were facing in Canada, mainly due to the lack of recognition of their education and work experience back home. Canada had welcomed them with the promise of a better life, but when they got here, the reality was something different. The Canadians who had been here for generations told me how they needed more support to enter the new digital economy but found most of the resources were going to newcomers.

This was not the Canada I remembered. Perhaps, it was because I was too young and idealistic when I left, and my memory was skewed. Or maybe it was because not only had things changed but I had changed as well. I raved about the multicultural Canada that I grew up in. A country that respected all cultures, whether newcomers, French-speaking Canadians, Canadians who had been here for generations, or First Nations peoples. They were all part of the cultural mosaic we called Canada. But something had been lost. It encouraged me to press on and knock on more doors.

At my office opening launch event, I stepped to the mic and announced I would be stepping down. The reason for this is an interesting story but perhaps for another book. I bring up my short-lived political career because it introduced me to an important community leader named Thambirajah Vasanthakumar, who I would come to know as Dr. Tham, the owner of Computek College.

With the late Dr. Thambirajah Vasanthakumar,
former owner of Computek College, 2015

The opportunity to acquire Computek College first came my way in 2008; I was still living overseas and not particularly interested. At the time, running a college in Canada didn't appeal to me in the slightest. I had other goals for my career. But then six years later, in 2014, Dr. Tham approached me about the opportunity again.

Dr. Tham had seen my commitment to the community when I was running for office. Most people who run for office start connecting with the community to get votes, but I like to think Dr. Tham saw something in me. I honestly wanted to help people but not everyone sees that and I can understand why. But, Dr. Tham was a community leader himself and I like to think it takes one to know one. He recognized that I had the community mindset that he was hoping to find in someone to take over the school and lead his team. He knew I was still feeling down from my attempt at politics, and he said, "There are many ways to serve. Perhaps Computek College is the path for you."

Computek College of Business, Healthcare, and Technology had three campuses at the time, two located in Toronto and one in Markham. It was focused almost exclusively on the Sri Lankan Tamil population, founded on the premise of educating newcomers for Canadian employment.

I was ambitious and I thought this was an opportunity to do something different, to serve a different community and expand my experiences. I understand why this college was so needed in our community because I had witnessed all of these amazing, highly educated, highly skilled immigrants coming into Canada. Many were not getting the job opportunities they deserved based on their experience, work history, and education. I also knew that many companies and organizations in Canada were looking for highly skilled, highly educated people, so there was a disconnect. Not just Sri Lankan Tamil people but immigrants from many countries.

I realized that Computek College was an opportunity to bridge this gap, and I was one of the few people around there who could really do that because I knew both worlds so well. It was obvious to me that this valuable population needed help to get established. So, I agreed to Dr. Tham's offer and began the process of purchasing the college.

My father and my brother, Lavan Srinarayanadas, both led the purchase. We each had a very different approach and philosophy about how things should be run. My father's managerial style was more traditional, and it fit the current demographic of our workforce. My brother was a doctor with training and experience in the US, and he was more modern, always looking for ways to streamline and use data to drive decisions. I was more in the middle, having the experience of working with my father, working in Asia, and understanding the need for modernity for Computek to grow to the next stage. My brother took the role of CEO, and I took the role of CSO, and my father was an advisor. In a sense, we were like a three-headed hydra.

I asked Lavan to share his perspective of our time working together to show how someone with a different mindset uses the EIA method. He said:

> While I was doing my clinical rotations in medical school, I kind of fell in love with the intersection of technology and clinical medicine. And I found a niche there. When I came back to Canada, we were quickly introduced to Computek. My brother had this great insight that the college could serve a larger population of new immigrants into Canada.
>
> The three of us were able to combine our expertise in understanding these communities and interpreting the trends in immigration, education, and employment. My dad had a more traditional approach. He would've rather focused on one single population, going deep and growing that market. I came in with the idea that digitizing as many processes as possible and collecting data on those insights would prove valuable to our growth. This would also allow for automation and quick expansion while minimizing the resources required to implement.
>
> Obviously, a few roadblocks happened as we went. My brother understood that we had to focus on building a business before we could really start to build a data asset. You can't build a valuable data asset from a student population of five or even a hundred people. You need thousands of

people, so we had to grow, and most importantly, diversify our student population as quickly as possible.

But we were doing it all from scratch. At one point I was the CEO answering phone calls, welcoming students, and sitting at the receptionist desk. My brother and I were cleaning toilets. We were teaching classes, photocopying, faxing documents, and doing everything that was imaginable at the school. And this was all happening around the same time as big life moments. I got married, my brother got married, and he quickly had a kid, but we were doing all of this at the same time. We had a number of bumps in the road that turned into major obstacles. It created a lot of arguments, but at the end of the day, we were a team that was trying to push in the same direction with different viewpoints.

Honestly, if we had digitized as quickly as I wanted, we would've failed completely. But we didn't fail because my brother had a more pragmatic approach that we ultimately adopted. He trusted the importance of the data and the need to be digitized, but first, we had to understand the population we were reaching out to. He focused on engaging with people in their community to great success. I learned to stop and interpret what we were learning before I acted.

Computek gave me one important insight that I continue to use today: You can't engage with everyone in the exact same way and expect the same result.

With my brother, Lavan Srinarayanadas, in Abu Dhabi,
at the U.A.E. Presidential Palace, 2022

Lavan isn't exaggerating when he says we hit some bumps in the road. We were so excited to scale the college; we made some huge decisions that nearly took us down. The first years were extremely, extremely difficult. And I'm understating it. On September 5, 2014, we signed the purchase and sale agreement. The Ontario Ministry of Education gave us control in July 2015, where we could officially make decisions, as the career college space is highly regulated. One of the first things that we did was move from a 1,500-square-foot location into a 20,000-square-foot location, which is a massive footprint and a huge cost.

But we wanted to make an impact. We wanted to show that we were thinking big. Our lease at the time was almost the entire revenue of the business when we bought it. We also hired more teachers and staff to handle what we hoped would be an influx of students which also cost more money.

Typically when you buy an organization, it goes a little bit down in terms of its revenue. I am proud that we never went below the revenue that the organization had in the past, but we tripled our expenditure going into this new place.

On top of all that, our first child was born a few months later, so I was so stressed about how to support my family. On July 13, 2016, my wife Dasha and I were up late. It was around midnight, and she had just finished feeding our daughter who was just a few weeks old. I was typing away, doing some work, when the alarms went off at the college campus. I looked at the cameras and saw the bailiff locking our doors with a chain.

The next morning, I went over and found a notice that stated we were so far behind on our rent that we weren't allowed back inside. I still have that notice as a reminder of the highs and lows of this journey. I was newly married with a child, had no money, was being chased by bill collectors and landlords, but I had to believe in this dream if I wanted to make it a reality.

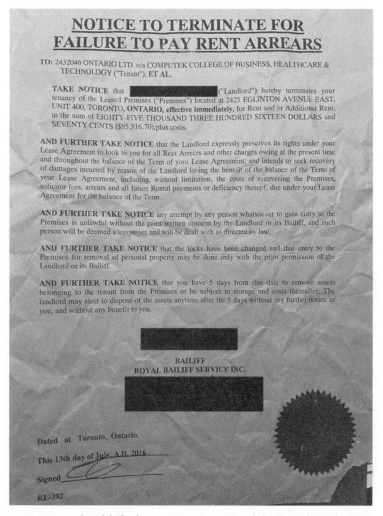

NOTICE TO TERMINATE FOR
FAILURE TO PAY RENT ARREARS

TO: 2432046 ONTARIO LTD. o/a COMPUTEK COLLEGE OF BUSINESS, HEALTHCARE & TECHNOLOGY ("Tenant"), ET AL.

TAKE NOTICE that ████████████ ("Landlord") hereby terminates your tenancy of the Leased Premises ("Premises") located at 2425 EGLINTON AVENUE EAST, UNIT 400, TORONTO, ONTARIO, effective immediately, for Rent and or Additional Rent, in the sum of EIGHTY-FIVE THOUSAND THREE HUNDRED SIXTEEN DOLLARS and SEVENTY CENTS ($85,316.70),plus costs.

AND FURTHER TAKE NOTICE that the Landlord expressly preserves its rights under your Lease Agreement to look to you for all Rent Arrears and other charges owing at the present time and throughout the balance of the Term of your Lease Agreement, and intends to seek recovery of damages incurred by reason of the Landlord losing the benefit of the balance of the Term of your Lease Agreement, including, without limitation, the costs of recovering the Premises, solicitor fees, arrears and all future Rental payments or deficiency thereof, due under your Lease Agreement for the balance of the Term.

AND FURTHER TAKE NOTICE any attempt by any person whatsoever to gain entry to the Premises is unlawful without the prior written consent by the Landlord or its Bailiff, and such person will be deemed a trespasser and will be dealt with as directed by law.

AND FURTHER TAKE NOTICE that the locks have been changed and that entry to the Premises for removal of personal property may be done only with the prior permission of the Landlord or its Bailiff.

AND FURTHER TAKE NOTICE that you have 5 days from this date to remove assets belonging to the tenant from the Premises or be subject to storage and costs thereafter. The landlord may elect to dispose of the assets anytime after the 5 days without any further notice to you, and without any benefit to you.

BAILIFF
ROYAL BAILIFF SERVICE INC.

Dated at Toronto, Ontario,

This 13th day of July, A.D. 2016

Signed _____

RL-392

Figure 3: A reminder of difficult times, 2016. I retrieved this from the garbage where I threw it that first day, knowing it would be a reminder to me one day of how far I came.

We were bleeding cash and bill collectors were calling. My first year of marriage wasn't going well at all due to the financial challenges. But by far the worst part of all of this was that I wasn't sure how I was going to take care of our daughter, Sofia.

You can't put on a sad face at work. When you lead, you have to lead with confidence. Yes, it's important to be open and honest and share the realities of the situation, but nobody wants the captain of the ship to say, "I don't know where the hell we are going" and start crying. I cried at home by myself in the bathroom. I also drank a lot, gained weight, but continued to push through. Winston Churchill once said, "If you find yourself in hell, keep going!"

My father reminded me at this time, "You have to believe. If you believe, nothing else matters because you will make it happen."

Dasha was struggling being a new mother in the middle of her residency in medical school and was off on maternity leave. There was a little income from her residency, but not much, which was also frustrating for her. I brought home nothing for years. In fact, I was selling all my assets and savings to keep the college afloat. There were many people other than my direct family who supported me during this time period.

One of the most critical factors to our survival was the commitment of our people. Mathi Kula, who led our accounts department, was not only a huge support as she managed bill collectors with whatever little money was coming in, she also lent us money to keep the college alive. Jeyan Ratnam, who managed our IT infrastructure from my family's days in Bangladesh, was also a constant support throughout this period. When your back is to the wall and everyone is looking to attack, it's the people who stand beside you who leave an impression on you for life. They remain to this day two of my most trusted advisors.

With Wazeer 'TJ' Jalal and Mathi Kula, one of my Special Advisors, 369 Global, 2022

Sofia saved me in more ways than she will ever know. She was a child, but she gave me the energy and joy that no one else could or wanted to.

An interesting note is that Sofia was born on June 21, 2016. June is the 6th month, 21 adds up to 3, and 2016 adds up to 9. So, her numbers are 369. A year later, I registered 369 Global, which would become our parent company, and station 369 was my production company. Dasha, with all her challenges with me at the time, lent me the money to start these businesses from her line of credit.

Why am I sharing all of these struggles? To emphasize that no one believed. No one believed in buying a college that served immigrants. No one thought a college could be led by immigrants. No one thought there was any business value in this college at all. Honestly, many people still don't.

How do you talk about a global perspective and the value immigrants can bring to a country during financial challenges like this? You don't. You need to survive first.

Lavan's insights highlight the importance of understanding and adapting to the unique needs of the communities we serve. He underscores the value of the EIA method to help us navigate the complex cultural landscape at Computek while making decisions that impact this new-to-us community and industry. As he mentioned, the first step that transformed Computek College from a failing school into the thriving institution it is today was the way we approached embedding ourselves in the community.

The first step we took was to diversify the business. We hired staff and instructors from different ethnicities. We also hired some team members who came from a more corporate educational institution. This is when the challenges began. We were so diverse in so many ways, the cultural clashes were tremendous. My father wanted to work with the original team and slowly scale the business, and my brother wanted a more corporate team to ensure we were moving into a modern way of operating the college.

Neither of them was wrong; it was just different directions. I wanted a mix of both. I wanted the cultural essence of what the original Computek offered under a corporate structure. For me, this micro challenge in Computek was the macro challenge we have in Canada and also the challenge we have globally as a global village. If we could work through the challenges in our diverse workforce at Computek, the solutions we would find could provide insights for Canada. And then, Canada could use those insights to lead the world.

However, I had to make a difficult decision: to continue to fight through the challenges of the cultural clashes or to start again. I used to be a competitive swimmer, and my coach, Coach Norm would tell me sometimes, "You have to take two steps back before you can take one step forward."

So annoying. I hated hearing that from Coach Norm. I hated coming to the realization that was what Computek needed to do. But it had to be done. I let go of several of our team members and began working with the original team to get sales through the door. This process was not pleasant. I was letting go of good people because I had made a mistake, not them.

Excited by the prospect of reviving Computek College, I was determined to understand the intricacies of the local community and the unique needs of the immigrant population we served. I quickly realized that the key to our success lay not in boardroom strategizing but out in the bustling streets of the Greater Toronto Area (GTA) where our students lived and worked.

To truly embed ourselves in the community, we took a hands-on approach. I taught communication classes to our students, which allowed me to gain firsthand insights into their perspectives, aspirations, and challenges as newcomers to Canada. Through direct interaction, I built genuine relationships and learned valuable lessons that would shape my leadership style and the direction of the college. Teachers are with their students for such a long time, so you get these little nuggets of insight just by being in their presence. This is opposed to, "Hey, fill out the survey and let me know what you think."

By teaching this course, I learned so much. In most cultures, we revere teachers. We call them gurus. A lot of people from my culture don't talk about the college or university they went to. Instead, they say, "I learned from this teacher."

This reflects the respect and reverence our students have for their teachers because they are the students' guides, showing them a whole new world.

As we immersed ourselves in the lives and experiences of our students and the broader community, we realized that interpreting cultural nuances would be essential to our success as an institution. We understood that culture is not just a set of traditions or customs but a complex web of values, beliefs, and ways of being that shape how individuals perceive and interact with the world around them.

One of the first cultural nuances we encountered was the diverse range of communication styles and preferences among our student body. Some students came from cultures where direct, assertive communication was the norm, while others were more accustomed to indirect, nuanced forms of expression. This diversity sometimes led to misunderstandings and conflicts. We learned through this observation that to address this, we were going to need to provide training to faculty and staff on cross-cultural communication skills like active listening, nonverbal cues, and cultural sensitivity.

Another distinction was the varying attitudes and expectations around education and career development. For some students, higher education was a deeply held value tied to family honor, while for others, academic pressure was a major stressor, especially when coupled with adapting to a new culture. We began to see the need for customized academic and career counseling services to support students in navigating these dynamics.

We also recognized how students' cultural backgrounds impacted their learning styles. Some preferred collaborative group environments, while others favored independent, self-directed approaches. Again, as we interpreted this information, we saw that we would need to create diverse educational opportunities like traditional classroom sessions, online options, experiential learning, and multimedia resources. There have been many wins and many losses, but it is slowly getting better and better.

We took a great deal of time defining who we were and who we served. This is a conversation that should happen in any organization in any new environment. I listened to my staff, and some of the suggestions they came up with drove the decisions we made and continue to make today.

Beyond academics, we sought to understand the cultural nuances in students' personal and social lives, such as juggling multiple responsibilities like jobs and family care, so that we could make informed decisions about related factors such as flexible scheduling, childcare access, transportation, and other holistic support services.

Finally, we recognized how trauma, mental health stigma, and cultural perspectives on issues like pain management and workplace dynamics could significantly impact our instructors' and students' well-being and success. This led to conversations on how we might be able to partner with healthcare providers and community organizations to offer culturally competent counseling, programming, and workplace integration training.

By deeply interpreting these nuances, we shifted away from a one-size-fits-all model toward more student-centered, culturally responsive education and support services. This cultivated higher engagement, performance, and a reputation as an institution that valued cross-cultural competence.

I have never been afraid of putting my name out front. God has given me the gift of speech, but to honor that gift is to match my actions with my words. I made videos as the CEO encouraging students to attend the college and talking about the things we were doing in the community. I attended trade fairs and events, and team members would join when they could, but many times, I stood by myself.

Prospective students who would come to the college would comment, "Hey! You're the guy in the videos." You couldn't buy the trust that was built in those days. I knew every student who came through the doors, and they knew me. We fought hard to help each other succeed; they focused on building their skills to enter a career they loved, and I focused on building a business that would provide them the skills and training they needed to succeed. It was a symbiotic relationship; it always has been and always should be.

It was around this time I met Kumaran Nadesan. Kumaran had started a nonprofit organization called "comdu.it" with some of his friends. The organization leveraged the talents of the diaspora to support the needs of their home country. It differed from other nonprofit organizations that focused on sending money back home or starting projects. On the contrary, comdu.it focused on knowledge sharing, which went both ways—to the home country and to the diaspora individual looking to reconnect with their roots. With Kumaran's focus on education and knowledge sharing on a global scale, our values aligned immediately.

Kumaran worked in the government at the time in several departments, so he had a good understanding of how government worked. He was also a great strategist and communication expert, so I sought his advice on how to position Computek in order to scale. I explained my background and my thinking around global talent and the value of immigrants. He encouraged me to double down on this idea and boldly show this through everything we did. Essentially, it was the early stages of building the brand of Computek and also my own personal brand, as it turned out.

We began using our students and staff members in the images and videos found on our website. Kumaran suggested participating in both government and private events where I could share my ideas and what I saw in the education space.

Our videos resonated with students and more of them came in. It was around this time I met Wazeer (TJ) Jalal. TJ was Computek's first international student about twenty-five years ago. TJ worked for Computek after he graduated and then went on to work for several other colleges until purchasing his own college and later selling it. He was now consulting for colleges to help them scale. TJ had met my father years ago when he was still working at Computek. TJ had heard about the challenges we were having at Computek and met with my father offering support. My father introduced me to TJ, and honestly at first, I was reluctant.

We had met so many consultants who claimed they could help, but all they wanted was money and provided no practical support. Most consultants would tell us, "We have to change several things before we could really make a change to the bottom line." The moment I connected with TJ was when he said, "You can't make any changes if you don't have any money. The first thing we need to focus on is cash flow." We aligned in focus and things started happening as we built on the momentum.

TJ joined as a consultant but later became our VP of student affairs and then the executive VP for Computek College. I couldn't have grown the business without him. It was important to have someone who understood the student experience because they went through it themselves. But also, it was important to hear the feedback and suggestions from him and others on our team to ensure we were defining policies and procedures that supported our students' journey. Understanding the journey of students like TJ and others on our team prompted us to make the decision not to charge additional fees for international students.

In Canada, the vast majority of educational institutions charge three and four times more for international students than they do for domestic students. In real numbers, for a $10,000 program, international students are charged $40,000. We don't do that at Computek College. It would be financially lucrative, but it goes back to how we want to be as a college. When we know the challenges international students face and we want to have a long-term trusted relationship with them. What would it say about us if we charged them more than others? Decisions like this come from awareness first and empowering those who share that knowledge to participate and implement those decisions second.

The end of 2017 marked the first year we broke even since I took over the college. That still didn't allow me to get paid, but it did give me an opportunity to take a Global Professional Masters of Law program at the University of Toronto.

With all these challenges why would I go into a master's program? There were several reasons. The first was fulfilling a personal dream of going to law school. I needed to do something for myself, and I felt this was something I would be proud of. Second, the insights I gained from this program helped me as a leader. The third reason was probably the most significant of them all. I wanted to understand the professional minds of Canadian culture. Similar to my MBA in Bangladesh, the program helped me understand the minds of business professionals in Toronto.

This was critical because the challenge I found was not with the students who were coming to the college. The challenge was the organizations that were hiring them. By completing these courses, I would gain insights and perspectives to better approach them with Computek graduates.

I graduated in 2018; the same year, my son Leonardo was born on November 18, 2018. My brother decided to attend a master's program at Georgetown University and was poached by one of the partners at Deloitte to work in their Washington D.C. office. He made the difficult decision to leave Computek, but we both knew it was the right decision for him and the ambitions he had for his career.

By the end of 2019, we had turned the business around. In fact, we had serious discussions with two other colleges for us to acquire them. Then, March 2020 was the start of lockdowns for Toronto and the beginning of managing a college through the COVID-19 pandemic.

Prior to March 2020, Computek prided itself on in-class learning. We did have online courses that supplemented in-class learning programs, but we insisted that the best way to learn was to come into the classroom. Incidentally, the online learning was a partnership I negotiated with Udemy in 2017; however, it wasn't going well because everyone thought, "Who would want to learn online?"

We ended the Udemy partnership by 2018 when we learned that 90 percent of students who took an online course didn't complete the program. During COVID, everyone only completed school online, but I recently read that post-COVID, 90 percent of students still aren't completing online programs.

During the pandemic, our first order of business was to determine our values so we could navigate through this new reality. We made the decision that no one was going to get fired. But we had to figure out how to move forward. The second order of business was training our instructors to teach online so we could keep the college running. I conducted the training workshops myself. The first Monday after the shutdown began, we submitted our plan to the ministry to get approval to deliver our programs fully online while I trained our staff. Two days later, on Wednesday, we received the Ministry's rejection letter—we could not teach online. We didn't get approved.

As a doctor in a hospital, Dasha was under tremendous stress. So was I. So were we all. I read the rejection letter in my garage before I went in the house. I cried. It's good to let these things out. Then, I leveled up and walked into the house. The next day, I continued training and we reapplied to the Ministry. By Friday of that first week, we received the permission to teach online. Entre-preneurship can be really fun.

Throughout the years, our business grew exponentially. While we slowed down a bit during COVID, we still grew. This is all thanks to the team and the efforts they put in to ensure we were still providing value to the students. We went from a college that enrolled fifty students a year to a college enrolling two thousand students a year.

As a result of our success/survival through COVID, we had many interested buyers and investors knocking on my door to purchase or invest in the college. I contacted third-party consultants to give me an objective picture of where Computek stood.

Computek College has several key licenses that are difficult to get, and after over thirty years in the education sector, Computek has built a strong reputation with students, employment partners, gov-ernment, and other stakeholders. But investors focus on the numbers and our growth is what attracted them the most. Our valuation from the time I purchased the college in 2014 has gone up by a factor of ten in ten years.

Post-COVID economic challenges continued for many people. Interest rates went up, inflation was on the rise, and housing prices in Canada soared, as did rent and groceries. It was and continues to be a challenging time. The minimum wage in Ontario, Canada as of 2024 is $17.20/hour. The living wage in the Greater Toronto Area (GTA) is $25/hour.

We made the decision not only in Computek but all entities within the 369 Global group to level up to the living wage for all of our team members. It's a heavy lift for the organization but an important one to recognize the contributions of our team and ensure we are there for them as they have been there for us.

EMBEDDING IN THE COMMUNITY

My mother was a registered nurse in the UK, but when she came to Canada, they asked her for her Canadian experience. At the time, my father was working overseas to support us, and my mom was raising us three kids. She enrolled in a private college in Winnipeg so she could be certified to work in daycares. She loved the experience of going back to school, and although she went to work in a daycare where there were more kids, she loved the independence and "adult time" it gave her while we were in school.

When I entered university, in one of my first classes, the person sitting beside me was my mom! She wanted to get back to university to get her bachelor's degree. There were many lessons I learned from her, but on this occasion, there are three things: (1) Age is nothing but a number, (2) Education is the great uplifter, and (3) My mom is tough as hell!

Having my mother around the college was a great help. Computek's student demographic is in the thirty-five to forty-five age range, 75 percent of our students are women, and they are predominantly newcomers to Canada. That demographic was my mom exactly when she first came to Canada. As a result, she related to students immediately. She helped connect with them in a way no one else could, which resulted in great student satisfaction.

I immersed myself in the lives of our students and I began to notice patterns that would inform our strategy. As I mentioned earlier, students came from cultures where direct, assertive communication was the norm, while others were more accustomed to indirect, nuanced forms of expression. Recognizing the potential for misunderstandings, I knew we needed to provide that important cross-cultural communication training for our faculty and staff to foster the most inclusive learning environment we could.

We also had to continue to take into account the varying attitudes and expectations around education and career development. For some students, higher education was a deeply held value tied to family honor, while for others, academic pressure was a significant stressor, especially when coupled with adapting to a new culture. To this day, we work hard to customize our academic and career counseling services to support students in navigating these complex dynamics.

To further embed Computek College in the community, we made a concerted effort to hire faculty and staff who reflected the diversity of our student body. We sought out individuals with firsthand experience of the challenges and triumphs of the immigrant journey, knowing they would bring invaluable perspective and empathy to their roles. By building a team that truly represented the community we served, we fostered a more welcoming and inclusive environment for all.

The process of embedding in the local community was not without its challenges. As a newcomer myself to this specific context and industry, I had to navigate cultural differences, build trust with key stakeholders, and earn the respect of our students and staff. However, the time and effort invested in understanding the local landscape would prove instrumental in Computek College's transformation and success.

Understanding the student population's needs was one thing. But there was a much larger challenge—getting Canadians to understand the value of the students.

I am a person who fits between cultures, not perfectly in them. As a third-culture kid, I have learned to navigate through multiple cultures and ensure my message is heard by communicating in a way that resonates with the culture I'm engaging with. It doesn't always happen the way I imagine it will right away. In fact, in most cases, it takes several failed attempts and learning before I am able to get my message across. But, it's something I have done throughout my life and this skill helped scale Computek College.

The other aspect of embedding was attracting our staff members to us and providing them with opportunities to embed themselves in our culture. Embedding goes both ways. TJ was from the community and understood better than anyone else the populations we served. He was fully embedded, so I couldn't think of anyone I'd rather have by my side as a decision-maker to work on policies at the college. It was the same with Priyo. I brought in my uncle and embedded him and others in the team, which helped us understand the communities and where the advantages of selling would be.

To be fair, this isn't a new thing. If you go into the e-commerce sector, you're going to find someone in e-commerce to help. But sometimes, people forget that the principle is applicable culturally. Bring in someone who knows that community but also ensure they have a voice in decision-making.

There are plenty of ways to get this wrong. After we expanded our campus, the next order of business was to create a diversified team. We hired instructors and staff from different communities and still others came from more corporate environments. This all took a toll on the way the school ran.

The corporate world has processes and structures that are very important if you want to scale very quickly. When I first bought Computek, I felt like we needed to bring the essence of diverse immigrant populations into Canada's corporate culture. So, I just went ahead and hired a bunch of very corporate people. I guess I figured if I could smash them together into a very ethnically run business, it would solve the problem. It was a complete failure. Not because those two things can't or shouldn't happen together. It's just that I didn't do it in the right way.

But if you look at Canada on a macro level, that's what is happening now.

It's like, "Hey, you immigrant, come here, take some kind of workshop and boom, fit into the Canadian workplace."

It doesn't work. I did that and I failed. Again, it doesn't mean the concept of immigration is wrong. It just means the way that we're doing it is wrong, and we have to change and pivot. For me, Computek continues to be a micro example of the challenges Canada faces as a nation and the challenges the world faces as we exist as a global village.

ACTING ON LOCAL INSIGHTS

As we continued to embed ourselves in the community and interpret the cultural nuances that shaped our students' lives, we realized that it was not enough to watch and learn. To truly make a difference, we needed to act on the insights we had gained and use them to drive meaningful change both within our institution and in the broader community.

One of my first priorities as the new CEO of Computek College was to diversify the student body. The college had previously focused primarily on the Sri Lankan Tamil communities, with 99.9 percent of the students and 100 percent of the staff coming from this background. Having grown up in Winnipeg and worked overseas, I appreciated the value of diversity and knew that it would be crucial to the college's success. Students need to experience a multicultural environment in a safe classroom setting because they are going to go into a multicultural environment in the workplace.

We began by actively recruiting students and staff from different communities and worked extensively with grassroots businesses that understood the importance of serving the community. As a result, the college's demographics began to shift, and we saw a significant increase in enrollment. From a student body of fifty Tamil students in a year, we grew to two thousand students from many different countries and cultures from all over the world in 2024. That was over a ten-year period.

Today, Computek's student population consists entirely of recent immigrants and newcomers to Canada. They are permanent residents, new Canadian citizens, and their age range is primarily between thirty-five and forty-five years old. Notably, 75 percent of our student base are women who find themselves in the middle of their careers, seeking to either upskill or secure a Canadian healthcare job after having held a similar position in another country.

Once these students enrolled, we had to effectively engage with their diverse communities. Leveraging the insights gained during the first two phases of the EIA method, we tailored our approach to celebrate their unique traditions and create an inclusive environment that prioritized making everyone feel welcomed and valued.

One of the first areas where we put these insights into action was in our curriculum development. By engaging with students, we realized that many of our traditional academic programs and courses were not fully meeting their needs. Some students struggled to see the relevance of certain subjects, while others felt the curriculum did not reflect their cultural values and perspectives.

We encourage students to participate in workshops, engage with the community at large, and help plan and organize partnerships within the community to further support these initiatives. An example of this is our financial literacy workshops. How do you do your taxes in Canada? How do you save for a mortgage? Why is your credit score important? There are some immigrants who come here with huge amounts of money and don't know what to do next, so we increased their awareness to access financial services.

Acting on these insights about the need for more diverse learning opportunities, we created workshops that complemented the courses our students were taking. For example, students would complete their accounting course, and we would add a workshop covering the latest developments in accounting and financial understanding in Canada.

We sought out opportunities to engage with the community in informal ways. We hosted cultural events and festivals on campus, celebrating the diverse traditions of our students. We also encouraged students and staff and anyone else to get involved in local initiatives like participating in financial literacy classes, presentations on healthcare options in Canada, and civic engagement workshops. For the latter, we wanted to ensure that people understood their right to vote and the importance of their voice as participants in their new democratic home. For some, voting back in their home countries was a dangerous life-or-death situation, so they had to be shown how and why they should vote. We reminded them that they're in this wonderful place called Canada where their voice needs to be heard. This built trust because it sent the message, "We believe in you, we want to inform you, and to educate you so that you can participate fully in your new home. It's not just a business. We care about you as individuals, and we want you to succeed here."

Beyond the curriculum, we took action to create a more inclusive campus environment. After hearing about the challenges students faced in balancing responsibilities, we implemented flexible scheduling with evening and weekend classes. We also expanded mental health services through culturally sensitive counseling partnerships, having learned about the stigma surrounding mental illness in some cultures.

Here you are coming and telling them, "Hey, this is how you open a bank account and we'll give you a $500 credit card." But they have $500,000 to put somewhere. It's just a mismatch because they just think all immigrants are people who come with no money and no resources. Our wealth management events brought in consultants from different banks and financial institutions who would come and chat with some of our students who were in that space. They were encouraged to start thinking about life insurance policies, how they could save for their kids and retirement. It was a great hit.

When we equalized tuition pricing for international and domestic students, we surprised a lot of people. This is an unheard-of action in our industry—we are one of only two colleges we know of that don't charge extra for international students. Some might view this as a sacrifice of hundreds of millions of dollars for the sake of principle, but we see it differently. In our culture, when you invite someone into your home to eat, you don't charge them. It's not a sacrifice; it's an opportunity to do what's right and combat the toxic practices that often target international students.

The same thing happened when we made our videos and used photos of ourselves and our students in our marketing material. People outside of Computek were taken aback. We want to feature regular people because that's who we serve—not models. No other college owners were creating videos like this at the time, and I still don't see anyone else doing it.

The results of our actions are beginning to emerge, and they are evidence that the EIA method works. In 2020, we hired a third-party consulting firm to analyze Computek and give us a report on how well we were addressing actual needs for our students and to make suggestions on what we could do better. The report stated:

> Over 95% of current students (n=324) expressed satisfaction with their education at Computek. Additionally, 54% said they were very satisfied when asked about its usefulness in helping them achieve their goals. Only about 3% expressed a neutral opinion. Graduates (n=72) shared similar sentiments; a total of 92% stated that they were satisfied, while 58% said that they were very satisfied... Among current students (n=324), 94% agreed that their studies at Computek provided them with relevant skills for the career they want, while 55% strongly agreed. Additionally, 94% of current students said they were confident that their program of study was for an in-demand role in the current job market. Among graduates (n=72), 87% agreed that they had graduated from a program that was in-demand in the current job market.[3]

We aren't perfect, by any means, but we are certainly working on improving and learning more every day. The journey of Computek College is one of continued evolution and dedication.

LOOKING FORWARD

Computek College today remains dedicated to deepening its integration within the GTA. The dynamic and diverse communities are flourishing, and we continue to be a part of it. Our commitment to community engagement is evident in our ongoing collaborations with

---

3   From a 2020 report titled, "The Future of Work in a Post-Covid-19 Era and the Impact on Newcomer Employment Outcomes" by Milieu Strategy and Consulting.

partners and other stakeholders, along with new initiatives aimed at enriching the local region. Upcoming partnerships with technology start-ups and community organizations will continue to bridge the gap between education and community needs, ensuring students not only learn but also contribute meaningfully to their surroundings.

In response to the rapidly changing job market, we are launching innovative educational programs focused on emerging technologies and industries. These programs are being designed to equip students with critical, future-ready skills in fields such as artificial intelligence, blockchain, and digital marketing.

There are whole societal trends in Canada. One example is that by some estimates, where six people were Baby Boomer managers at any given institution, we now have one person who is a Gen Xer or a Millennial taking over the role of those six people when they retire. And in many instances, that one person doesn't really want to do it because they want to be a digital nomad and not participate in society. This is the problem.

So, how do we address that? It's going to be extremely challenging. Let's look at the media industry as an example. It was very much print-focused. And we hired a team of people who, because they've been in the industry for so long, are very highly paid and have large pensions.

I was actually going to buy a media institution that was going bankrupt here in Canada, but my financial advisor cautioned me strongly to leave it alone. To let it go bankrupt. Why? Because if I bought that institution, I would carry the liability of all of these highly paid people who would soon be looking for pensions. The digital economy today, although very exciting, doesn't pay the same as print and cannot afford all the high salaries and pensions of the past.

In nearly every industry, the old business model of significant infrastructure and a mega workforce is no longer relevant, and it's difficult to pivot to new models of business. The concept of what they were doing is not wrong. It's just they've gone so far and it's so expensive that they cannot take that same team into this new, low-cost reality. This is the challenge.

The same thing happens in education. The problem here is that education as a whole has changed. Gone are the days when people were very interested in coming to the classroom to learn. There's still a great interest, but the population that is coming into the classroom has decreased.

Online learning is great if you want to upskill or broaden knowledge, but you probably don't want a surgeon who is going to operate on you who only took an online course, right? So, why would we think that this is going to be the future? It is a part of the future, but we aren't putting all of our eggs into one basket.

Educational institutions in Canada and around the world are finding the percentage of students who are coming into the class has reduced, and yet we continue to have these highly paid professors and instructors who are still working on the old model. In contrast, schools are not earning the same level of revenue in the new model of education.

How do you take this great infrastructure that we have with these massive buildings and campuses and move it into this new world? I think it's going to be very challenging.

As we begin to get into global education and training in a new B2B (business-to-business) model, it is helpful to remember that educational institutions, including Computek, have traditionally focused on a B2C (business-to-consumer) model. This means we train our students and that is the end. They are the end-user and on their own to find jobs after they graduate. A new way of looking at education is called work-integrated learning.

It means as one of the executives and decision-makers for my college, I want to have a relationship directly with future employers of my students so we can train specifically for those employers. Let's look at the accounting program that we have at Computek, as an example. If somebody wants to hire an accountant at the New York Knicks basketball team and somebody else wants to hire an accountant at the New York Public Library, they have different needs. The accountant whom you want to work for a basketball team has a different set of soft skills than the accountant whom you want in the New York Public Library.

But the old model expects that we are creating an accountant who can serve both. That's not the case.

In many instances, the educational institutions are selling their name. This accounting course is at NYU Stern, or this course is taught at Harvard, or this course is taught at the University of Toronto. It is that brand that brought value, not the fact that the graduates from this program fit the specific needs of, say a library or a basketball team.

We are going to change the way education approaches this problem. To do that, we are going to set up specifically for, say, the needs of the New York Knicks. We will embed ourselves and interpret what we find out before we act. Maybe we will find out that their turnover for accountants is two to three years and that they have a very specific set of needs. By partnering with us to design a program specifically suited to their needs, we can provide them with two new accountants every year. They're going to pay whatever tuition it is to train these two accountants, and we are going to ensure that we get them the best-suited people we can. That's the B2B model.

We are in the process of applying these insights to Computek College. One of our programs trains personal support workers (PSWs). These students essentially learn how to be a nurse's assistant, which is critical in our healthcare system and long-term care facilities.

Hospitals are always hiring PSWs and there are never enough. As a result, agencies were created that offer a pool of trained PSWs. When healthcare institutions are short-staffed, they reach out to an agency to fill that role. The problem is that Canada has a decreasing population, which means there are not enough people to train and help fill empty positions so institutions continue to work with agencies to close the gap.

This is where it gets problematic. If a healthcare institution hires a PSW from an agency, they have to pay the agency for that PSW. Let's say they pay the agency $100 an hour for that PSW. The agency then pays that PSW $30 an hour for their work for the entire time that they work at that institution. If the average employment period is two to three years, that healthcare institution is paying thousands of dollars to an agency that doesn't offer any value beyond the initial placement. And we wonder why our healthcare system is crumbling.

Computek is interpreting what we have learned. We are partnering with an organization in the long-term care industry that hires about 150 PSWs in any three-year period. We went to the institutions and said, "Look, you're going to get your PSWs from all over the place. Why not contract with us to ensure that you have 150 PSWs every three years, and we will customize their training to suit what you need? We can create training programs for PSWs to learn your specific software systems, programs, equipment, and policies. Rather than paying an agency that only gives you a random PSW, you can pay for our students' tuition because it's a hell of a lot cheaper than paying a hundred dollars an hour for three years. That's $70 an hour that you can save once their training is over."

Computek makes money, the tuition is paid, and the students are happy because they know if they hit all the targets of the program, they are going to be hired at this institution. This is the model that we are creating, and we believe all educational institutions should do the same. It is a partnership directly with employers, with educational institutions, and training partners. This is the future of education.

By staying ahead of educational, workplace, and technological trends, the college will ensure its curriculum remains relevant and its students are well-prepared for the challenges of tomorrow.

CHALLENGES AND LESSONS LEARNED

Transforming Computek College was not without its challenges. One of the most significant hurdles we faced was navigating that initial integration of a diverse team. I mentioned earlier that when we first acquired the college, we brought in a group of experienced corporate college operators to work alongside the existing staff, who were primarily from immigrant backgrounds with a small business mindset. We naively believed that these two groups would quickly and easily come together, but the reality was far more complex.

The clash of corporate and small business cultures led to significant difficulties. Some staff members left the organization, while others resorted to legal action against us. We found ourselves in severe debt, unable to pay vendors, and facing the very real possibility of failure. In hindsight, it's clear that our approach to integrating these two distinct cultures was a major misstep.

This experience taught me a valuable lesson about the importance of cultural sensitivity and the need for a gradual, thoughtful approach to change management. We had to learn to listen more closely to the concerns and perspectives of our staff, and to find ways to bridge the gap between our corporate goals and the realities on the ground.

Celebrating Computek College's Graduation, 2023

The heart of any educational institution is its instructors (gurus): Top Row L – R: Swetha Srikanthan, Johanna P Grant, Pamela Mutombo, Muraly Srinarayanathas, Wazeer 'TJ' Jalal, Ashique Rahar, Veenah Selvakumar, Gulnar Kuramaeva

Middle Row L – R: Hamsathvani Ratnesh, Varshini Sivanesarajah, Betina Zulu, Perveen Kanwal, Huma Abbas, Nazmul Islam, Savithiri David, Annies V Jose

Bottom Row L – R: Arceo Cabaneros, Dr. Berhe Goitom, Tamirat Temespen Alemneh, Daniel Demoz, Barun Bakshi, Rezene Haile Ghebreghiorghis, Mohammed Azarudeen Hanifa, Priyanka Sharma, Ghulam Yahya Shareef

Another key challenge I faced was my own personal growth and maturity as a business leader. When I first took on the role of CEO at Computek College, I was eager to prove myself and to make my mark. I had grand visions of rapid expansion and transformation, but I quickly realized that I lacked some of the skills and experience necessary to lead such a complex organization.

Over time, I learned to be more patient, to listen more than I spoke, and to surround myself with experienced mentors and advisors. I also came to understand the importance of long-term thinking and relationship building. In the early days, I was often focused on short-term gains and quick wins, but I soon realized that lasting success requires a commitment to the long game.

Perhaps the most important lesson I learned through my experience at Computek College was the need for adaptability and resilience in the face of adversity. There were moments when I doubted myself and questioned whether I had made the right decision in taking on this challenge. But I also learned that setbacks and failures are an inevitable part of the entrepreneurial journey, and that what matters most is how we respond to them.

Through it all, I remained committed to the EIA method and to the principles of community engagement, cultural competence, and student-centered learning that had guided our work from the beginning. And while the road was not always smooth, I am proud of what we accomplished at Computek College and the lives we were able to impact along the way.

Looking back, I can see how my experiences at Computek College helped to shape my approach to business and leadership in profound ways. I learned the importance of understanding and respecting cultural differences, of building strong relationships based on trust and mutual understanding, and of staying committed to a vision even in the face of adversity.

These lessons have stayed with me in the years since, guiding my work at 369 Global and beyond. And while I know that there will always be new challenges to face and new obstacles to overcome, I am confident that the skills and insights I gained at Computek College will continue to serve me well, no matter where my journey takes me next.

As I was writing this book I was thrilled to learn that Computek College achieved a spot on Canada's Top Growing Companies ranking by The Report on Business Magazine 2024.

This reinforces further the Embed-Interpret-Act (EIA) Method. Computek is deeply embedded in the communities its campuses are located in, allowing it to actively engage at a grassroots level with a broad range of stakeholders—from government to industry and community. The information that Computek accesses through such an embedded engagement has allowed us to make pragmatic interpretations of the rich insights gained about the challenges and expectations that our students have about why, what, and where they want to pursue the right training that can help them become competitive in an ever-changing labour market. These interpretations have then led to Computek making strategic, innovative, and values-based business decisions that we have acted upon with great agility resulting in the rapid growth the college has experienced since 2020.

Let the beauty of
what you love be
what you do.
—RUMI

CHAPTER 8

369 GLOBAL

I REGISTERED 369 GLOBAL in November 2017 without knowing what I wanted to do other than I knew it only made sense if I started to think global. By the end of 2017, I had burned through all my savings and sold off every asset I could in order to keep Computek College afloat.

The end of 2017 marked the first year that we broke even since I had purchased the college in 2014. I was thirty-eight and in the middle of my Masters of Law at the University of Toronto, and I could see very clearly that no one thought as I did. But I didn't let this get to me. Pablo Picasso said, "Every act of creation begins with an act of destruction." This was certainly the case for me during this period of my life.

People are always amazed at the growth of Computek College. We grew ten times over a period of ten years, bringing with that growth a financial success to be proud of, surely. However, the greatest achievement for me in those years lies in my newfound awareness, acceptance, and desire to embrace diversity.

At 369 Global, we are diverse not only in ethnic origin—currently representing over thirty ethnicities—but also in age. Our students are in every decade of life, from twenty to seventy. Our staff brings a wide variety of work experience, from new graduates to corporate executives and from entrepreneurs to government and nonprofit organizations.

Celebrating with the 369 Global team, Mini-Con, April 2024

Can you imagine the conversations in our head-of-department meetings at Computek College between a thirty-year-old and a seventy-year-old about the future of education and how we should position ourselves as a college? Or imagine the conversation of someone who has spent decades in government and another with those same decades spent as an entrepreneur? The outpouring of ideas is amazing as they think about our go-to-market strategy as we expand into new countries.

There's an African proverb that says, "If you want to go fast, go alone. If you want to go far, go together." We are living that every day at 369 Global.

But it didn't start that way. In 2017, I was still focused on ensuring Computek would be self-sustaining. In 2020, I engaged Kumaran Nadesan as a consultant to help me brand the college the right way. I had started volunteering with Kumaran and his organization, comdu. it, with a few other friends at the university he was attending.

As I mentioned earlier, comdu.it was a nonprofit focused on connecting the diaspora with their homeland to do a knowledge exchange. Many nonprofits at the time were focused on sending money back home or starting projects in their home countries, but comdu.it was focused on connecting talented students to projects in their home countries that needed their skills. In turn, the students returning home would have a greater and richer understanding of their roots.

The strategic lens Kumaran put on tapping into the diaspora and thinking globally aligned with my global thinking. He also encouraged me to promote our focus on serving and hiring immigrants on our website and marketing material.

Our friendship grew, as did our business success. In 2023, he became my co-founder at 369 Global. His years of experience in government and working with diaspora communities was a great asset and matched my international entrepreneurial journey.

We solidified our vision to educate, inform, and activate global thinkers.

STRATEGIC VISION

In today's world, there is significant focus on inward-looking policies and what is happening within the borders of our societies. Despite the recent step back from globalization, I believe that we have already passed the point of no return. While I support nation-building and the development of strong nations, especially in the context of living and benefiting from multicultural Canada, the concept of a global village is here to stay.

The reasons for this are numerous. We have a global communication tool called the internet and a generation that increasingly travels and works globally, beyond borders. We also have global payment systems like bitcoin and decentralized structures like blockchain. As we think about the future, it is likely that we will dig deeper into these global structures.

It is crucial for us to address global issues, such as the management of vaccine distribution during a global pandemic, as we are not going to turn away from globalization; we are only going to go deeper. We need to establish regulations and safeguards and come to a consensus as a global community on our rules of engagement. This is an ongoing process, just like the work of multiculturalism in Canada. We are in the midst of globalization, and while we may be at a challenging point on the learning curve, we must continue to push forward to overcome these challenges and benefit society as a whole.

The challenges we face in 2024, with violent eruptions around the world, are indeed difficult and with valid positional points of view. However, from a global perspective, violence is not the answer. We must prioritize the well-being of children and the elderly, as the quality of a society is often measured by how it treats these demographics. As we face an aging global population and consider the impact of our actions on the environment, it is essential to reflect on these questions, as they serve as metrics for how we value our world and the quality of life we create.

Canada became an independent nation on July 1, 1867. Then, in 1947, the Citizenship Act was created. Thirty years later, in 1977, dual citizenship was introduced. This opened the path for Canadian multiculturalism. In this single act, Canada as a nation not only formalized its multicultural policy, it led the way through action by allowing people to keep their first passport while still holding a Canadian one. I believe this is the reason why it has been said that the Canadian diaspora is the only diaspora that accurately reflects the demographics of the world.

After living in so many countries, I am happy and proud to be living in Canada. As an entrepreneur, the opportunities here provide a huge advantage. Unlike other nations, we are Ethiopian Canadians, Ukrainian Canadians, Tamil Canadians, etc. It is not about our culture coming first, but rather a recognition that our culture is a part of the larger Canadian multicultural mosaic. It's not just First Nations and French-speaking Canada, as some people who don't live here imagine we are. It is a rich tapestry that reflects all of the people on our planet.

But how does all of this relate to business and 369 Global?

Not only do we find people from all over the world here in Canada, but there are also Canadians all around the world. I spent some time in Africa for a 369 Global project, and I was surprised to learn the owner of the hotel I stayed in was the cousin of one of our staff members. When one of our team members went to Vietnam for another project, he was guided by a Vietnamese Canadian, who is one of the lead educators in Canada for the hospitality industry.

When foreign start-ups want to enter the North American market, they come to Canada. Why? Canada is a great soft landing before entering the US market. It is also a great test case to understand world consumer habits because the world is here and encouraged to continue to embrace and celebrate their traditions. If you want to expand globally and enter a market you're not familiar with, it is not hard to connect with someone from that region in Canada.

John Stackhouse was the former editor and chief for The Globe and Mail newspaper in Canada and now sits as a senior VP in the Royal Bank of Canada's think tank arm. In 2020, he published a book called Planet Canada. In it, he highlights the almost three million expats from Canada of whom the majority lead global organizations because Canadians have a unique ability to bring diverse people together. He observes that non-Canadian leaders can easily identify Canadians because they ask the right questions and listen to the answers.[4]

William A. MacDonald wrote the book, Might Nature Be Canadian, in which he wrote the following:

> Mutual accommodation is about co-operation, compromise, and inclusion. It helps to get things done by making room for others, though some pressure or force might be needed along the way. It strengthens, not weakens, identities. In an ideal world, everyone would be a winner. Mutual accommo-dation makes that outcome more possible. Throughout its history, Canada has exhibited a stronger drive toward mutual accommodation than any other country—an approach that has allowed its increasingly diverse citizens to live together peacefully and successfully, even as they retain their own culture, language, and religion.[5]

---

4   John Stackhouse, *Planet Canada* (Toronto: Random House of Canada, 2020).

5   William A. MacDonald, *Might Nature Be Canadian* (Montreal: University of Toronto Press, 2021).

As we look to educate, inform, and activate global thinkers at 369 Global, there is no stronger base than Canada. Canadians by nature are global thinkers. As a nation, Canada encourages this mindset, which, in my opinion, is our greatest asset. We offer global strength and mutual understanding. Canada and Canadians can lead the world with this strength.

369 IN ACTION

At 369 Global, we are actively exploring new markets and opportunities around the world to expand our impact and reach. Our recent efforts to establish new partnerships and programs in countries like Kenya, Vietnam, Malaysia, and Indonesia exemplify how we are embedding the EIA method into our global strategy and operations.

Cyber Guard Africa Ltd., Startinev & 369 Global's Africa Hack-a-thon, United States International University-Africa, Kenya, February 2024

Through empathy, we first seek to deeply understand the local context, culture, and needs of each market we explore. Rather than assuming our existing programs and approaches will immediately resonate with others, we invest significant time on the ground—meeting stakeholders, listening to different perspectives, and building trusting relationships. For example, before launching cybersecurity training in Nairobi, our team engaged over six hundred participants to gauge interest and tailor the program. In Vietnam, we learned that gaps in hospitality and tourism training were the most pressing issues, requiring us to pivot from our initial plans.

These interactions provide valuable insights that inform how we adapt and localize. We realized that what works in Toronto often needs modification to succeed in Hanoi or Nairobi. Local partnerships, like the MOUs we signed with Vietnamese universities, are key to co-creating relevant programs. Respecting cultural nuances, down to pronunciation of key phrases, is essential to building credibility. Recognizing how workforce needs differ across markets allows us to focus on the right mix of technical and soft skills.

Armed with insights gained, we then begin the action to launch and scale new initiatives. In Kenya, this meant delivering a hybrid training program to hundreds of students eager to access our offerings. In Vietnam, we are now working toward a fall launch of our first hospitality program, with plans to expand to other disciplines over time. Across all locations, we are investing in multilingual staff and customized content to ensure we deliver the high-quality, contextualized education 369 Global is known for.

In addition to training, 369 Global worked in partnership with St. Joseph's Communication Media to launch 3 magazine in Canada and to the world. Our understanding of the world is woven from the myriad cultures we've embraced, the languages we have spoken, and the lands we call home. 3 talks about our identity not as dictated by a single culture or location but as a mosaic of our experiences, relationships, and travels. The magazine prioritizes stories that resonate beyond borders and celebrates people who live beyond boundaries.

3 magazine, launched September 2024

While ambitious, our global expansion is rooted in the fundamentals that drive success in our home market—a keen understanding of student and employer needs, a willingness to continuously learn and adapt, and an uncompromising commitment to quality and impact. By marrying this student-centric mindset to the EIA method, we aspire to bring the "secret sauce" behind our Canadian success to new frontiers. Just as important as the programs we deliver is how we conduct ourselves in each new geographic location—with cultural sensitivity, humility, and a genuine desire to co-create value with local partners.

Our global journey is still in its early chapters, and we will undoubtedly face new challenges and complexities as we scale. However, with the EIA method as our north star—continuously pushing us to listen, learn, and localize—we are confident in our ability to make a meaningful difference in the lives of students and communities worldwide. The 369 Global team is more energized than ever to bring our model of high-quality, market-driven training and education to new markets—empowered by the knowledge that doing so will require embracing diverse perspectives and ways of working. This is the opportunity before us and one we intend to pursue with focus, passion, and integrity in the years ahead.

Yesterday I was clever, so I wanted to change the world. Today I am wise, so I am changing myself.

—RUMI

CHAPTER 9

EIA IN ACTION

IN PREVIOUS CHAPTERS, we explored the concept of the EIA method and how it can be applied in various business and educational settings to drive business expansion success, cultural competence, community engagement, and social impact. Through the case studies of First Global Data, Priyo Communications, and Computek College, I wanted to show the transformative power of this approach in action, as organizations embedded themselves in diverse communities, interpreted cultural nuances, and acted on local insights to make positive impact and more fully succeed as we enter new markets.

As my friend, CEO of the Institute for Canadian Citizenship, Daniel Bernhard said, "There is definitely a value in business, I believe, of seeking out and embracing approaches that are exogenous to the marketplace—that come from someplace else. Because a competitive edge in any marketplace is basically a new approach to doing something."

One test of any methodology can be its ability to be adapted and applied across a range of contexts and challenges. In this chapter, I will go a little deeper into two examples of how the EIA method was put into practice in the realms of event planning and healthcare training.

Through these case studies, I hope to illustrate how the EIA method can be used to break down barriers, build bridges, and create more inclusive and equitable communities. As I participated in these initiatives, I was able to gain key lessons and insights. I share this in the hopes that it will further inform our efforts to drive positive change in our personal and professional lives.

I invite you to reflect on your own experiences and challenges as an entrepreneur and to consider how the EIA method might be applied in your own context. Whether you are an educator, a health-care professional, a business leader, or simply someone who is passionate about making a difference in your community, this method is applicable anytime you expand into unfamiliar territory.

HOME AND GARDEN SHOW

Another powerful example of how we applied the EIA method at Computek College was through our involvement in Veedu Living as a Home and Garden Show. This single event showcased the latest trends and products in home decor, gardening, and lifestyle. It provided a unique opportunity for us to embed ourselves in the community, interpret cultural nuances, and act on local insights in a new and exciting way. Veedu is the word for "home" in Tamil, so it made sense to use it in the name of the show.

The idea for the Veedu Home and Garden Show first emerged through our conversations with students and community members. As we embedded ourselves in the local South Asian community, we began to hear a common theme: many people felt that the existing home and garden shows in the area did not reflect their cultural values, preferences, or aesthetics. Similarly, Western companies who sold home and garden products didn't think South Asian markets would be a market for them.

Recognizing the potential for this event to fill a significant gap in the market, we began to explore the idea further. We conducted market research, reached out to potential vendors and sponsors, and started to develop a vision for what the Veedu Home and Garden Show could be.

As we got deeper into the planning process, we continued to interpret the cultural nuances that shaped the preferences and behaviors of our target audience. We learned that many South Asian households placed a high value on multigenerational living, with grandparents, parents, and children often sharing the same home. We also learned that South Asian culture placed a strong emphasis on hospitality and entertaining, with large gatherings of family and friends being a common occurrence.

Based on these insights, we began to tailor the show to the specific needs and preferences of the South Asian community. We recruited Western vendors and exhibitors who offered products and services to engage specifically with the South Asian community. We designed the layout of the show to accommodate larger family groups, with wider aisles and more seating areas to encourage socializing and interaction.

But as we continued to plan the event, we also encountered some unexpected challenges. Some of the vendors and exhibitors we approached were not used to catering to a South Asian audience and struggled to adapt their sales and marketing strategies accordingly. Vendors just didn't know how to connect with audience. We had to show them how to do this, culturally speaking. We noticed that some exhibitors were using aggressive sales tactics that were off-putting to many attendees, while others were not effectively showcasing the cultural relevance of their products.

To address these challenges, we once again turned to the EIA method. We provided cultural competence training to exhibitors and vendors, helping them to understand the unique preferences and communication styles of South Asian consumers. We also worked with them to develop culturally relevant marketing materials and product displays that highlighted the ways in which their offerings connected to South Asian culture and values.

Also, we noticed there was no ethnic representation in the creative agency space at that time. People didn't understand the demographics they were serving, so we saw an opportunity for us, leading to the creation of a new creative agency.

The impact of these efforts was significant. As the Veedu Home and Garden Show launched, we saw a tremendous response from the South Asian community. Attendees raved about the culturally relevant products and services on display and appreciated the welcoming and inclusive atmosphere of the event. Exhibitors and vendors also reported high levels of engagement and sales, with many expressing a newfound appreciation for the importance of cultural competence in their business practices.

But the impact of the Veedu Home and Garden Show extended far beyond the event itself. As word of the show's success spread, we began to receive inquiries from other event planners and businesses seeking to learn more about what we were doing.

Why was this significant? Regular downtown home and garden shows typically attract around 10,000 attendees over a weekend, while rural shows outside the downtown core draw about 1,000. The Veedu Home and Garden Show, by comparison, had an impressive 4,500 attendees. We were able to track this data through surveys and raffle draws that required participants to visit a certain number of booths. Vendors who paid extra ensured that attendees came to their booths, allowing us to monitor which products were purchased. This data-driven approach, while not as sophisticated as today's methods, provided valuable insights into our target market's preferences and behaviors.

Perhaps even more significant was the realization that many companies had no idea how to effectively target and engage with South Asian and immigrant communities. They were surprised to learn that these communities were actively seeking out their products and services. Recognizing the untapped potential, these companies approached us for consultation, marketing plans, and partnerships to enter this market successfully.

One notable example was T-fal, the well-known cookware company. They had a booth at the Veedu Home and Garden Show and were impressed by the event's success. Recognizing the untapped potential, T-fal approached us to pitch ideas on how we could collaborate to better reach the South Asian market. As I examined the creative agencies in the Greater Toronto Area at the time, I noticed a lack of diverse leadership and a limited understanding of ethnic markets, despite having some employees of color on their teams.

Seeing an opportunity to fill this gap, I pitched a more ethnically focused approach that differed from their current strategies. Although we didn't secure the T-fal contract, this experience sparked the idea to start our own creative agency. We had been experimenting with marketing and digital marketing at Computek College, so we had a good understanding of what worked on a smaller scale. There was a clear need in the market for companies seeking guidance to reach diverse communities. The T-fal experience demonstrated the importance of not only recognizing the potential in ethnic markets but also having the cultural understanding and expertise to effectively engage with these communities.

The success of the Veedu Home and Garden Show not only led to the creation of our creative agency but also paved the way for other ventures, such as our film production company and, ultimately, the establishment of our parent company, 369 Global. This demonstrates the power of the EIA method in business—by embedding ourselves in the community, interpreting cultural nuances, and acting on insights, we were able to identify untapped opportunities and expand our reach.

The EIA method is not limited to a one-way cultural exchange. Just as many Western companies have successfully taken their products and services to the East, such as Tim Hortons and KFC, there are also examples of Eastern concepts thriving in the West, as with Red Bull, the popular energy drink, which originated in Thailand. The creator of Red Bull recognized its potential and secured global rights to the product, leading to its massive success worldwide.

COLLABORATING WITH TRI-COUNTY MENNONITE HOMES

Another relevant example of the EIA method in action is our ongoing collaboration between 369 Global and Tri-County Mennonite Homes (TCMH). This partnership illustrates how embedding ourselves in local communities, interpreting cultural nuances, and acting on insights can drive meaningful change and create innovative solutions to complex challenges.

The story began when I traveled to Kenya with Steven Harrison, the CEO of TCMH. We went in conjunction with Talent Beyond Boundaries, 369 Global, other healthcare partners, and the local partner, JumpStart.

Dr. Steven Harrison, CEO, Tri-County Mennonite Homes, makes a guest appearance on my podcast, Third Culture Leaders, *May 2024*

With the team from Talent Beyond Boundaries, Tri-County Mennonite Homes, World Education Services (WES), SkyHive, Refuge Point, at UNHCR Refugee Camp Kakuma, Kenya, October 2023

Our mission was to find PSWs and entry-level staff to work at TCMH in Canada. The Canadian immigration program at the time had a specific initiative that benefited refugees in Kenya, providing a pathway for them to come and work at TCMH. My role was to assess the skills and training of potential candidates to ensure they met the needs of TCMH.

During our visit, we were amazed by the dedication and experience of the Kenyan PSWs. Despite working in hospitals with limited resources—reminiscent of a World War II movie with just bed frames and IVs—these individuals were performing exceptional work across various departments, from emergency to cardiology. They had gained invaluable experience due to the staffing shortages in Kenya but lacked exposure to modern medical technology.

Recognizing the potential of these skilled workers, we devised a plan to bridge the gap. 369 Global is now building a 1,500–2,000 square foot training facility within TCMH in Canada, equipped with the same medical equipment used in their actual work environment. Here's the game-changer: we are replicating this exact facility in Kenya, creating a mirror-image training center directly connected to TCMH.

By doing so, we are enabling Kenyan PSWs to train on the same equipment they will use when they start working at TCMH in Canada. This "Learn to Earn" model ensures a seamless transition, preparing them for success in their new roles. The beauty of this approach is its scalability—we can establish similar training centers in Ukraine, France, China, Bangladesh, or anywhere else in the world.

These micro learning centers serve as a cost-effective alternative to the massive infrastructure of traditional educational institutions. Universities like NYU Stern or the University of Toronto can leverage our global network of Learn to Earn centers, renting the facilities to conduct training, assessments, and even virtual job interviews with employment partners.

The EIA method is at the heart of this innovative approach. Embedding himself in the Kenyan context, Steven Harrison gained invaluable insights into the local healthcare system and the untapped potential of PSWs there. By interpreting the cultural nuances and challenges faced by these skilled individuals, we were able to develop a tailored solution that bridges the gap between their experience and the requirements of working in a Canadian long-term care home.

However, simply bringing Kenyan staff to Canada is not enough. Steven understood that integrating a significant number of new Kenyan employees into TCMH would require a thoughtful approach to ensure a smooth transition and cultural understanding. Drawing from his own experiences living and working in Rwanda during a time of crisis, Steven recognized the importance of creating a supportive environment that fosters cross-cultural collaboration.

To facilitate this integration, 369 Global is actively recruiting team members from the African continent who have worked and lived in both African and Canadian contexts. These global thinkers, some of whom are Kenyan themselves, possess a deep understanding of the cultures involved and are uniquely positioned to bridge the gap between TCMH's organizational culture and the incoming Kenyan staff.

By embedding ourselves in the local context, interpreting the cultural nuances, and acting on these insights, we are creating a model that not only benefits TCMH and the Kenyan PSWs but has the potential to revolutionize the way we approach international recruitment and training in various industries.

As we continue to refine and scale this model, we are excited by the possibilities it presents for fostering global collaboration, creating opportunities for skilled individuals from diverse backgrounds, and ultimately driving positive change in communities around the world.

THE TAKEAWAYS

These examples prove that the EIA method is not just a theoretical framework but a practical and adaptable approach that can be applied in a wide range of contexts and challenges. Whether we are seeking to improve patient outcomes in healthcare, celebrate cultural diversity in our events and experiences, or drive social change in our businesses and institutions, the EIA method provides a roadmap for success.

At its core, the EIA method is about listening deeply, learning humbly, and acting boldly. It requires us to step outside of our comfort zones, to engage with communities that may be different from our own, and be willing to challenge our assumptions and biases. It demands that we approach cultural differences not as barriers to be overcome but as opportunities for growth, innovation, and connection.

Through the partnership with TCMH, I learned how this approach could be used to bridge the gaps between students and healthcare institutions. The insights we gained led us to create a more technically competent and responsive healthcare workforce. By embedding ourselves in the communities of both the employer and prospective employee, interpreting our observations, and acting on the insights we gained, we are now designing curriculum and putting programs in place that enrich everyone involved.

Similarly, through the Veedu Home and Garden Show, I saw the power of the EIA method in celebrating cultural diversity and driving business innovation. By deeply engaging with the South Asian community, interpreting their unique preferences and aesthetics, and acting on these insights through a carefully curated event experience, we were able to create a platform for cultural exchange, entrepreneurship, and community building. The success of the Veedu Home and Garden Show not only demonstrated the business case for cultural competence but also highlighted the potential for the EIA method to be applied in new and exciting ways.

I am reminded that the work of building more inclusive and equitable communities is never truly finished. There will always be new challenges to face, new communities to engage with, and new opportunities for growth and learning. By embracing the principles of the EIA method— embedding ourselves in the lives of those we serve, interpreting the rich tapestry of cultural nuances that shape our world, and acting on these insights with courage and conviction—we can continue to drive positive change and create a brighter future for all.

My hope is that we can all take the lessons to heart and apply the EIA method in our own lives and work. I hope we can seek out opportunities to engage with diverse communities, to listen deeply to their stories and perspectives, and to act on these insights in ways that create meaningful impact. This means we must be willing to challenge ourselves, to step outside of our comfort zones, and to be agents of change in a world that so desperately needs it.

I really like what Nayeem Ali said about this:

I have an MBA in finance and I did a lot of strategy for AT&T before I started my own company. I used to manage planning, strategy analysis, and mergers and acquisitions. In my career, I have established relationships in Europe, Asia, Africa, and we are now launching all our technologies globally. Nothing has changed. It is the same mantra. Make sure you have the right talent. People are on the ground in those parts of the world who are embedded, and who understand the environment.

This method is about leveraging local talent and leveraging local experience to be able to have a strategy that works in that particular region in a shorter period of time. If you understand the environment you're operating in and understand what the wants and needs are of those partners you are looking to bring on board with you, then it makes it easier to put together a plan that works for both parties.

A lot of times when you look at business, the attitude is, "I have to beat that person. I have to be better than them."

But then someone else will say, "Well, I'm going to try to beat you and get a better deal elsewhere as well."

One of the things I've learned is that it's not about you or your division winning. It's about everyone winning. It can't be one wins, one loses. It has to be a win-win for both because when everyone wins, it is better for everyone.

In the end, the transformative power of the EIA method lies not just in its ability to drive business success or social impact, but in its capacity to bring us closer together as human beings. By embracing cultural differences as opportunities for connection and growth, we open ourselves up to the richness and beauty of the world around us, and we create the conditions for a more just, compassionate, and inclusive society.

CONCLUSION

THANK YOU FOR reading my book. Time is a precious gift and I appreciate you taking the time to read my story.

I am very grateful for the life I have lived so far and hopeful for the future. Yes, I have had challenges in my life and in my business, but I have always had great love and support around me to see things through. With these great blessings comes a great responsibility to give back to those who gave so much to me.

We have the choice to do many things in life and in business. I hope that this book will inspire you to take the time to get to know the people and places where you do business. In the corporate world, the focus was once on the shareholders. Now, it has transferred to stakeholders, which also includes the community around us. Please take the time to embed yourself in the community you serve and the community that serves you. Taking the time to understand each other provides the space and time needed to interpret the world around us with empathy and love.

The knowledge we gain from embedding ourselves and the inter-pretations we make in the world around us. The interpretations we make do not necessarily lead to the right action every single time. Often, the right action takes courage. Sometimes, while we know what the right thing is, it's easier not to do it. If you are a leader, we all need you to do the right thing because waiting for the person behind you to do it means no one ever will.

I had the opportunity to attend a workshop by Harvard Professor Thomas J. DeLong on authentic leadership, a remarkable event led by a remarkable man. Prof. DeLong took us through a series of exercises and case studies. During one of the exercises, he challenged us to think about our purpose statement, something that reflected our purpose in life. To help us, he said it is usually helpful to think of something in your childhood where you were in your zone—where time was not a factor.

He shared a story of one of his students whose purpose statement was "be with the frogs." This phrase brought her back to her childhood on a farm where she would go to her pond and play with the frogs for hours. If, during her career, she ever felt lost, she would look at her purpose statement to "be with the frogs." If she didn't feel that same fascination and delight with her work that she did as a child with those frogs, she knew she was in the wrong place.

After hearing this, I thought back to my childhood to a place where I felt in the zone, where I felt like my true self. I used to love to put on shows when I was young. Whether it was plays or songs or dancing, I loved performing. My favorite was magic shows. But every time I did a trick, I took great pride in showing my audience how I did it. That was the best part!

My purpose statement is: I am a magician who loves to teach people the tricks.

I love to wow people. I love to strive to do the impossible and make it possible. But as I do these things, it is just as important for me to show people how to do what I do. I hope I have shown you a few tricks that will help you on your journey in life and in business.

All the very best to you, my friend.

With Appa at St. Joseph Communications celebrating the official launch of
3 magazine on his birthday, January 27, 2024

In 2012, for my father's sixtieth birthday, I bought a major share in Sylhet Royals, a cricket team in the Bangladesh Premier League. What else do you buy the guy who taught you everything you know?

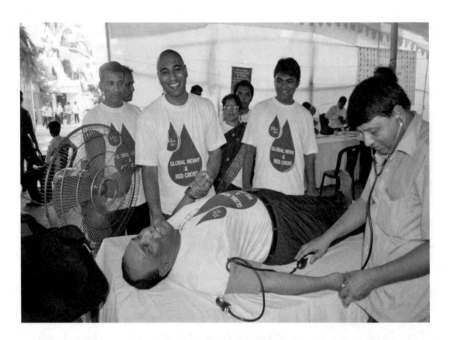

Global Neway, our company in Bangladesh, held the record at the time for the largest number of blood bags—three hundred—donated in a single day to the Red Crescent (Red Cross). This speaks to philanthropy and the spirit of giving back to the community that my father instilled in me.

My mom was a key supporter for me at Computek. As a former nurse, not only could she teach some of the healthcare courses, but also she went through the very journey our students go through … and she inspired the students to keep going.

For many years we all lived in different countries: Mom in Toronto, Kalpana law school in Manchester, Lavan residency in Chicago, Appa in Bangladesh, and me between them all. This picture is from 2013 and for a few years, we lived in the same city (Toronto) once again.

*Jaffna, 2023, at my family home where my father grew up and I had my first
birthday. It was a blessing to visit with my parents and my children.*

Training for my first marathon in 2022 with my son, Leonardo.

My extended family gathered on my fortieth birthday.

My parents and my daughter, Sofia, celebrated with me at my graduation from my Global Professional Masters of Law at the University of Toronto.

I like to experiment and try a lot of different things. I thought I'd test my standup comedy chops at Second City in Toronto.

Acting is one of my passions and I was in the cast of the film, This Place, *that premiered at Toronto International Film Festival (TIFF) in 2022. With my production company, station 369, I was also a producer on this film.*

Entrepreneurship isn't about things happening overnight. Sometimes it's years of experimenting, failing, and experimenting again. It's not about the win or loss, you have to love the journey. In 2002/2003 (I was 23/24), I created my first magazine in Bangladesh.

In 2023 I was on the cover of a magazine, Canadian Immigrant, *in Canada.*

In 2024, I launched my own magazine in Canada called 3.

With Professor Yunus and Queen Sofia of Spain at the Social Business Conference, Bangladesh. With us are Tafsir Awal and Ahad Bhai. From left to right: Professor Yunus, me, Queen Sofia, Tafsir Awal, Ahad Bhai.